Quotations from Abraham Lincoln

Dear David Spears —

  May anyone who reads this book
help to promote the qualities of character
that Abraham Lincoln possessed.

— Ralph Y. McGinnis

July 28, 1983

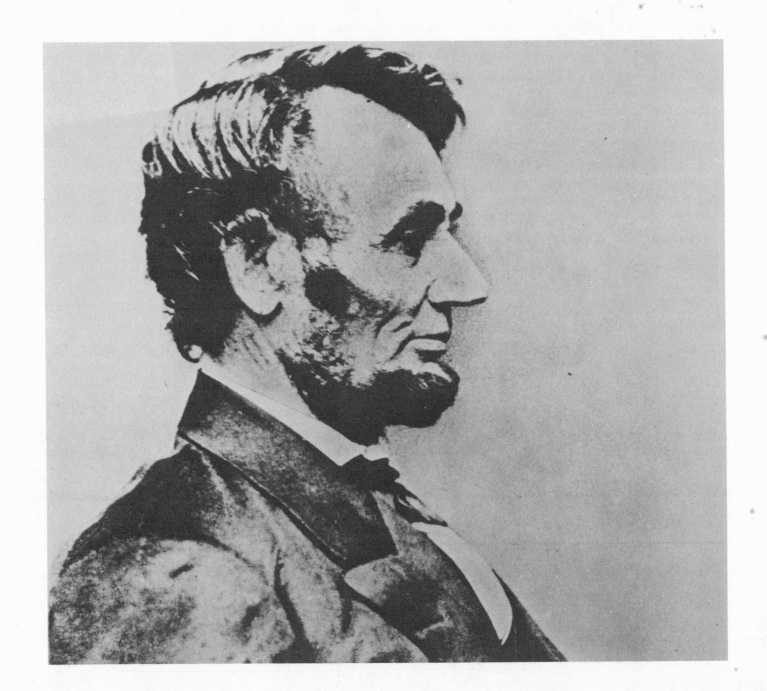

Quotations from Abraham Lincoln

Edited by
Ralph Y. McGinnis

Nelson-Hall
Chicago

Acknowledgments

So many persons have given encouragement and recommendations during the writing of this book that the recognition of only a few means the slighting of many. However, special acknowledgment must be made for the support received from Illinois Bell Telephone Company for permission to print the picture of the Lincoln-Douglas Debate at Alton, Illinois; the Illinois State Historical Library for permission to reprint all the other pictures and illustrations in the book; Mr. Tom Vance, Superintendent of the Lincoln Log Cabin State Park near Charleston, Illinois; Mr. Al Banton, Superintendent of the Lincoln Home National Monument, Springfield, Illinois; Dr. Beryl F. McClerren, Professor of Speech Communication, Eastern Illinois University; and Helen Betty McGinnis, my wife, to whom this book is dedicated.

Frontispiece — known as "the famous Lincoln profile," this photograph was taken in Washington, D.C. on February 9, 1864, by Anthony Berger who was manager of Mathew Brady's Gallery. A companion photograph, made at the same sitting, and the photograph were used in 1909 to model the Lincoln-head penny. *Courtest of the Illinois State Historical Library, Old Capitol Building, Springfield, Illinois.*

Endsheet photograph by Anthony Berger, who worked in Mathew Brady's Gallery, Washington, D.C., was made on February 9, 1864. A sketch from this picture was engraved on the United States five-dollar bill. Courtest of the Illinois State Historical Library, Old State Capitol, Springfield, Illinois.

Library of Congress Cataloging in Publication Data

Lincoln, Abraham, Pres. U.S., 1809-1865.
　Quotations from Abraham Lincoln.

　Bibliography: p.
　Includes index.
　1. Lincoln, Abraham, Pres. U.S., 1809-1865—Quotations.
E457.98.L558　　1977　　973.7'092'4　　77-24595
ISBN 0-88229-316-8 (hardbound)
ISBN 0-88229-507-1 (paperback)

Copyright© 1977 by Ralph McGinnis

Manufactured in the United States of America.

Contents

Illustrations

The seventh and last of the Lincoln-Douglas debates was held in Alton, Illinois on October 15, 1858.

The above photograph was made of a painting which was commissioned by the Illinois Bell Telephone Company for display throughout Illinois. *Courtesy of the Illinois State Historical Library, Old State Capitol, Springfield, Illinois.*

Preface

As Americans began the last quarter of the Twentieth century, they sensed that impending national chaos could only be averted by finding some kind of inspirational leadership for all phases of their complicated form of living. A sudden turn of interest, somewhat nostalgically, at the beginning of our Bicentennial celebration, to the trials and tribulations of our founding fathers, seemed to indicate that Americans were honestly searching for a new, perhaps old, concept of leadership and inspiration.

In a time of national trial, where can America find new faith, new hope, new brotherly love, new policies, and new inspirational leadership for the future? The character of Abraham Lincoln is a model of virtue which could serve as a guide for solving the problems in the United States during our Bicentennial year of 1976 and beyond.

As president of the United States during the tragic Civil War, Abraham Lincoln has been written about more often than any other leader in the world except perhaps Jesus of Nazareth. In devotion to his convictions on civil liberty, national unity, and reconstruction with amnesty, Abraham Lincoln was ridiculed and vilified as severely as any other president before his time. As a leader whose intelligence, wisdom, and judgment on all matters of human relations have stood the test of time, Abraham Lincoln has become the most frequently quoted president in United States history.

Historians readily quote Lincoln on a multitude of political, economic, and social issues. Most Americans, on reading or hearing one of those quotations, generally react with pride for their country and with respect for Lincoln. But they quickly forget the exact wording of the quotation, and they seldom keep a record of where they can find the quotation at a later time. Furthermore, most Americans do not possess the many volumes containing the complete works of Abraham Lincoln. And even if they did possess them, the locating of a particular quotation could constitute a problem.

The one great challenging philosophy today to American democracy is the ideology of political and economic totalitarianism. In Western Europe that philosophy had been propounded by the writings of Karl Marx. In Eastern Europe, Nikolai Lenin formulated the theoretical and political concepts under which the Union of Soviet Socialist Republics developed. In Communist China, a little book labeled *Quotations from Chairman Mao Tse-tung* has become the official guide for thought and action of all Chinese people. Young Chinese today, by fluently reciting quotations from their national leader, delight in displaying their knowledge of and devotion to the Great Proletarian Cultural Revolution in China.

Americans could profit greatly from studying, and even memorizing, quotations from the writings and speeches of one of our greatest leaders and believers in civil liberty and free enterprise. For such a purpose, a ready resource book on the philosophy and spirit of America would be: *Quotations from Abraham Lincoln.*

Tributes to Abraham Lincoln

Throughout the world, leaders of renown have given high praise to the character of Abraham Lincoln. A few of those tributes are:

Not often in the story of mankind does a man arrive on earth who is both steel and velvet, who is as hard as rock and soft as drifting fog, who holds in his heart and mind the paradox of terrible storm and peace unspeakable and perfect. Here and there across the centuries come reports of men alleged to have these contrasts. And the incomparable Abraham Lincoln, born 150 years ago this day, is an approach if not the perfect realization of this character.
>   —Carl Sandburg, American poet and biographer, addressing the Joint Session of Congress, February 12, 1959.

Abraham Lincoln belongs not only to the ages, but to all humanity. Immortality is his in the hearts of all who love freedom, everywhere in the world.
Each year two million people visit the Lincoln Memorial in Washington, D.C.
In New Delhi, India, a Lincoln Society is establishing a museum in his honor.
High school students in Tokyo last summer ranked Lincoln as the most respected of all world figures.
>   —President Dwight D. Eisenhower, addressing the National Sesquicentennial Dinner in 1959.

Abraham Lincoln was at home and welcome with the humblest, and had a spirit and a practical vein in the times of terror that commanded the admiration of the wisest. His heart was as great as the world, but there was no room in it to hold the memory of a wrong.
>   —Ralph Waldo Emerson, American poet, essayist, and philosopher, 1876.

I confess that the more I learn of Lincoln's life, the more I am disposed to look at him much as my mother and those early freedmen did, not merely as a great man, not merely as a statesman, but as one to whom I can certainly turn for help and inspiration as a great moral leader in whose patience, tolerance, and broad human sympathy, there is salvation for my race, and for all those who are down but struggling to rise.
>   —Booker T. Washington, American Negro educator and former slave on the 100th anniversary of the birth of Lincoln.

Of all the great national statesmen in history, Lincoln is the only giant.
>   —Leo Tolstoi, eminent Russian novelist.

Now his simple and weighty words will be gathered like those of Washington, and your children and your children's children shall be taught to ponder the simplicity and deep wisdom of utterances which in their time, passed, in party heat, as idle words. . .
> —Reverend Henry Ward Beecher, American preacher and President Lincoln's part-time special Ambassador to Great Britain, in eulogy, 1865.

Where did Shakespeare get his genius? Where did Mozart get his music? Whose hand smote the lyre of the Scottish ploughman, and stayed the life of the German priest? God, God, and God alone; and as surely as these were raised up by God, so was Abraham Lincoln; and a thousand years hence, no drama, no tragedy, no epic poem will be filled with greater wonder, or be followed by mankind with deeper feeling than that which tells the story of his life and death.
> —Henry Watterson, noted editor of the Louisville Courier-Journal, addressing the Lincoln Union, Chicago Auditorium, on Lincoln's Birthday, February 12, 1895.

His Gettysburg speech is not surpassed, if equaled, in beauty, simplicity, force, and appropriateness by any speech of the same length in any language. It is the world's model in eloquence, and condensation.
> —William Jennings Bryan, American statesman, in 1909.

Honors did not change him and pride could not corrupt him. Yet he could rise in the dignity of his manhood to a majesty that has not been surpassed by any ruler of any people under any form of government.
> —Chief Justice Charles Evans Hughes of the United States Supreme Court in 1909.

Now he belongs to the ages.
> —Edwin M. Stanton, secretary of war in the Lincoln Cabinet, spoken at the bedside when President Lincoln died.

The Character of Abraham Lincoln

From the foregoing tributes, and from the great wealth of literature written about him, a long list of attributes can be compiled depicting the character of Abraham Lincoln.

Listed at random, the following references to Abraham Lincoln may be considered as favorable evaluations of his character: "his strong sense of duty"; "Lincoln's great sense of fairness"; "unchanged by honors"; "The uncorruptible Lincoln"; "the dignity of his manhood"; "his splendid strength of character"; "the greatest ruler in the world"; "the Great Emancipator"; "Honest Abe"; "the best railsplitter"; "his skillful genius"; "inspired idealist"; "a great moral leader"; "a diligent student"; "the lonely giant among statesmen"; "a forgiving man"; "a man of great human sympathy"; "his humility before God and man"; "his Christian charity"; "a patient man"; "a man of fundamental principles"; "a great moral leader"; "his broad human understanding"; "his leniency"; "the deep wisdom of his words"; "a man of generosity"; "his methodical analysis"; "his pitiless pursuit of truth"; and "the savior of the Union."

Any man with the convictions and courage that Abraham Lincoln possessed was bound to make enemies with a vocal portion of society. Accordingly, low evaluations of Lincoln have included such phrases as "the original Illinois gorilla," "the bumbling idiot," "cheap politician," "uncompromising dictator," "ignorant," "selfish egotist," "the white supremacist," "a puppet, " and "hustling politician."

In the multitude of attributes to Abraham Lincoln, the high qualities of character that occurred most often seemed to fall naturally into three general areas which dealt with aspects of his ethical character, his mind, and his basic beliefs.

The ancient Greeks evaluated a statesman's total effectiveness by analyzing his three qualities of ethos, logos, and pathos.

Ethos, or the totality of his character, included the goals, ambitions, motives, attitudes, initiative, responsibility, perseverance, truthfulness, and total philosophy of the statesman.

Logos, in ancient Greece, included all aspects of a man's mental processes, including: his inborn intelligence (or his intelligence quotient), his basic assumptions (assumed truths or major premises), his use of evidence, and his use of logical reasoning.

The *Pathos* of a leader not only included the kinds of emotional feelings that he embraced (out of the fifteen emotional appeals as identified by Aristotle), but also included the motives for his actions.

The inductive process of determining the major qualities of Lincoln's character resulted in duplicating the same three general qualities of human character that the ancient Greeks identified in their statesmen. Accordingly, memorable quotations from Lincoln's speeches and writings, as reported in this treatise, could be organized under the following headings:

Quotations representing Integrity (ethos)
  Quotations on Truth
  Quotations on Ethics
  Quotations on Work
  Quotations on Responsibility

Quotations representing Intelligence (logos)
  Quotations on Logical Thinking
  Quotations on Government
  Quotations on Economic Enterprise

Quotations representing Idealism (pathos)
  Quotations on Freedom
  Quotations on God
  Quotations on Forgiveness

The earliest known photograph of Abraham Lincoln was taken by N. H. Sheperd of Springfield, Illinois, in 1846. At that time Lincoln was congressman-elect from Illinois. *Courtesy of the Illinois State Historical Library, Old State Capitol, Springfield, Illinois.*

Quotations on *Truth*

Knowing the truth and living the truth was the quality that characterized the early manhood of Abraham Lincoln. His determination to be truthful was revealed through several incidents while he was working as a storekeeper in New Salem, Illinois.

On one occasion, when young Abe Lincoln discovered that he had overcharged a customer by six cents, he walked several miles after he closed the store to return the overcharge. On another occasion, he sold a half pound of tea in the darkness of late afternoon. The next morning he noticed that he had used a quarter pound weight on his scales instead of the half pound weight. Whereupon he closed the store and delivered the extra quarter pound of tea to the customer. These incidents and others earned him the nickname around New Salem of "Honest Abe."

I am not bound to win, but I am bound to be true. I am not bound to succeed, but I am bound to live up to what light I have. I must stand with anybody that stands right, stand with him while he is right and part with him when he goes wrong.

The above quotation is the one most often repeated from Abraham Lincoln on the subject of truth and honesty. Lincoln himself stated that concept in various adaptations on many occasions, as at Peoria, Illinois, October 16, 1854.

Lincoln's Peoria Speech of October 16, 1854 was delivered by prearrangement after U.S. Senator Stephen A. Douglas had spoken for three hours in defense of his authorship and passage of the Kansas-Nebraska Act of 1854. That act had established popular sovereignty for Kansas and Nebraska territories, and had repealed the Compromise of 1820. Lincoln stood for restoration of the Compromise of 1820 and admitted that by doing so he might be classified along with Abolitionists who stood for certain proposals with which Lincoln did not agree. As Lincoln stated:

Some men, mostly Whigs, who condemn the repeal of the Missouri Compromise, nevertheless hesitate to go for its restoration lest they be thrown in company with the Abolitionist. Will they allow me as an old Whig to

3

tell them good-humoredly that I think this is very silly? Stand with anybody that stands RIGHT. Stand with him while he is right and PART with him when he goes wrong. Stand with the Abolitionist in restoring the Missouri Compromise; and stand AGAINST him when he attempts to repeal the fugitive slave law. What of that? You are still right. In both cases you oppose the dangerous extremes. In both you stand on middle ground and hold the ship level and steady. In both you are national and nothing less than national.

Honesty was the first quality of character which Lincoln considered that every lawyer should possess. In his Notes for A Law Lecture written on July 1, 1850, Lincoln stated:

There is a vague popular belief that lawyers are necessarily dishonest . . . Let no young man choosing the law for a calling for a moment yield to the popular belief. Resolve to be honest at all events; and if in your own judgment you cannot be an honest lawyer, resolve to be honest without being a lawyer. Choose some other occupation, rather than one in the choosing of which you do, in advance, consent to be a knave.

During the one term that he served as a United States Congressman, Lincoln opposed the continuing of the Mexican War beyond the objectives stated in the original United States declaration of war. By opposing the campaign to capture Mexico City, he appeared to disgrace himself as a "friend of the enemy." Back home in Illinois, public meetings were held to denounce him. Nevertheless, in Congress when the Ashmun Amendment was introduced condemning President Polk for unnecessarily begin-

ning and continuing the war, Congressman Lincoln voted for it. In desperation, William Herndon, Lincoln's law partner back home in Springfield, wrote to Lincoln to tell him that he was committing political suicide. In his letter of February 1, 1848, Mr. Lincoln answered by writing:

Would you have voted what you felt and knew to be a lie? I know you would not. Would you have gone out of the House-skulked the vote? I expect not. If you would have skulked one vote, you would have had to skulk many more before the end of the session.

In 1858, in a contest for an Illinois seat in the United States Senate, Mr. Lincoln contributed to his own defeat by asking the controversial Question Number 2 at the famous Freeport Debate. The question invited Senator Douglas to explain how a territory before becoming a state under Douglas's plan of popular sovereignty could exclude slavery from the territory. The question also enabled Douglas to give a qualified answer and thus win reelection. At the end of the campaign, although Lincoln was supported by a larger popular vote, Douglas was elected to the Senate by the state legislature. Following his defeat, Mr. Lincoln, in his letter of December 8, 1858, to his friend H. D. Sharpe, wrote the following:

I think we have fairly entered upon a durable struggle whether this nation is ultimately to become all slave or all free, and though I fall early in the contest it is nothing if I shall have contributed in the least degree to the final rightful result.

On many occasions President Lincoln was beset

by quarreling government officials who claimed that they had been slandered by fellow officeholders. When General Halleck, through the office of Secretary of War Stanton, requested that the postmaster general be removed from office for alleged slanderous remarks against certain military officers, the president wrote to the secretary of war on July 14, 1864 stating:

Whether the remarks were really made I do not know. If they were made I do NOT approve them; and yet, under the circumstances, I would not dismiss a member of the Cabinet therefore. I do not consider what may have been hastily said in a moment of vexation, at so severe a loss, is sufficient ground for so grave a step. Besides this, TRUTH is generally the best vindication against slander.

On July 4, 1864, Mr. Lincoln, as president, refused to sign the Wade-Davis bill allowing for retribution and punishment against a crumbling Confederacy. When he was informed of threats of assassination if he refused to sign the bill, he spoke as follows to the assembled senators who were pressuring him to sign:

If they choose to make a point upon this, I do not doubt that they can do harm. At all events, I must keep some consciousness of being somewhere near right. I must keep some standard or principle fixed within myself.

As in all confrontations with his opponents, President Lincoln acted as he believed was honest and true, even in the face of threatened assassination.

This picture, reportedly made in six different cities, probably was taken in Peoria, Illinois, by R. M. Cole in 1858. *Reprinted by permission of the Illinois State Historical Library, Old State Capitol, Springfield, Illinois.*

Quotations *on* Ethics

Closely akin to Abraham Lincoln's foremost quality of honoring truth and honesty was his high regard for ethical conduct. As Mr. Lincoln often explained, just being technically and legally right is not enough. A person needs to be morally and ethically right as well.

Sometimes Mr. Lincoln refused to take certain cases at law because, while they could be won easily on legal or technical grounds, they would violate certain ethical principles. One such story pertained to a potential client who asked Lincoln to represent him in collecting $600 to which he had a perfect legal claim. That story, as related by renowned Lincoln actor Richard Blake, represents attorney Abraham Lincoln speaking as follows:

Well, Jesse, you have a good case in technical law, and we can without a doubt win it for you. But we can also set a whole town at loggerheads, and furthermore we can distress a widowed mother and her six fatherless children. And—we can get for you $600 to which you seem to have a perfect legal claim, but which rightfully belongs as much to the widow as it does to you.

Now you must remember that some things that are legally right are not necessarily morally right. You will have to get some other lawyer to win this case for you. All the time that I would be in front of that jury, I would be saying to myself: "Abe Lincoln, you're a liar." I'm afraid that I might say it right out loud.

Now I will give you some advice for which I will charge you nothing. You seem to be a strong, able-bodied man, and I advise that you try to make $600 in some other way. And now, good-day.

As a lawyer, Mr. Lincoln sometimes was accused of "impoverishing the bar" because he did not charge fees as high as some of his fellow lawyers. Very often his fee was set in relation to the ability of his client to pay. He defended this practice as being basically ethical. Occasionally he charged nothing at all for his services, as in the case of his defense of Duff Armstrong in the Armstrong murder case.

Of equal irritation to many of his lawyer friends was Lincoln's desire to settle cases out of court even though, by so doing, he worked himself out of potential fees. It was part of Lincoln's sense of ethics.

In the notes that Lincoln prepared on July 1, 1850 for his lecture on law, Mr. Lincoln wrote:

Discourage litigation. Persuade your neighbors to compromise whenever you can. Point out to them how the nominal winner is often the real loser— in fees, expenses, and waste of time. As a peace-maker, the lawyer has a superior opportunity of being a good man. There will still be business enough.

In a world of conflict between standards of truth and principles of necessity, Lincoln was adamant in taking a primary stand which he believed was ethical even though it violated a secondary conviction. For example: Lincoln believed that slavery was morally wrong and that eventually it must be eliminated from the nation. He also believed that with civil war raging between the North and the South, preservation of the union was immediately more necessary than immediate liberation of the slaves. In his letter to Horace Greeley, famous publisher of the New York Tribune, on August 22, 1862, less than one month before he issued the preliminary Emancipation Proclamation, Lincoln defended his position:

I would save the Union. I would save it by the shortest way under the Constitution. The sooner the national authority can be restored, the nearer the Union will be "the Union as it was." If there be those who would not save the Union, unless they could at the same time save slavery, I do not agree with them. If there be those who would not save the Union unless they could at the same time destroy slavery, I do not agree with them.

In that same letter to Horace Greeley on August 22, 1862, Mr. Lincoln defended the ethics of a man who changes his convictions on controversial issues. In reference to his own possible change of mind he wrote:

I shall try to correct errors when shown to be errors; and I shall adopt new views as fast as they shall appear to be true views.

The ethics of President Lincoln's policy of reconstruction with amnesty was stated most forcefully in his Last Public Address on April 11, 1865. Although he was under severe attack because of the leniency of his policy in accepting Louisiana back into the Union, he defended his policy by asserting:

We all agree that the seceded States so called, are out of their proper practical relation with the Union; and that the sole object of the government, civil and military, in regard to those States is to again get them into that proper practical relation. I believe it is not only possible, but in fact, easier, to do this, without deciding, or even considering, whether these states have even been out of the Union, than with it. Finding themselves safely at home, it would be utterly immaterial whether they had ever been abroad.

Cheering crowds had swarmed in front of the White House on that early spring evening of April 11, 1865, demanding a victory speech. The message that President Lincoln delivered was disappointing. The ethics of his policy of reconstruction with amnesty could not be fathomed immediately by the mob that wanted vengeance against a defeated South. Pleading with the people to accept his ethical approach to the great problem before them, the president implored:

Let us all join in doing the acts necessary to restoring the proper practical relations between these states and the Union; and each forever after, innocently indulge his own opinion whether, in doing the acts, he brought the States from without, into the Union, or only gave them proper assistance, they never having been out of it.

Throughout his administration as president, Abraham Lincoln stood soundly on his fundamental belief in freedom and his unswerving belief in forgiving wrongs committed in human affairs. In overall reflection on his basic principles of life, and on his application of principles to specific plans for reconstructing the Southern states, he concluded in his Last Public Address:

No exclusive and inflexible plan can safely be prescribed as to details and collaterals. Such exclusive and inflexible plan would surely become a new entanglement.

Having stood on the fairness of different specific plans for the different states to be readmitted into the Union, Mr. Lincoln then concluded his statements on the ethics, the basic rightness, of his general policy by asserting:

Important principles may, and must be inflexible.

A somewhat humorous, and yet beautiful, example of Mr. Lincoln's application of ethics in the practice of his profession as a lawyer is contained in the following story of how he handled an unwanted case of law between a debtor and a creditor.

On one occasion in Springfield, a wealthy creditor asked Lincoln to bring a lawsuit against a poverty-stricken debtor for $2.50. Mr. Lincoln advised the creditor to let the whole matter drop, saying:

You can make nothing out of a lawsuit against him. Besides, it will cost you much more money to collect the debt than the size of the debt.

The creditor could not be persuaded and he announced that he would seek the services of some other attorney. Whereupon Mr. Lincoln said:

Well, if you are determined that a lawsuit should be brought, then I will bring it and prosecute the case. But my charge to you will be $10.00.

The creditor paid the fee and departed. Mr. Lincoln then left his law office and filed the suit in court. Next he hunted up the debtor, explained to him what had been done, and gave him half of the $10.00 fee. Together they went over to the Squire's office where the debtor confessed his debt and paid the bill.

The day ended happily for everyone: for the creditor who saw justice rendered and who recovered the debt; for the debtor who paid his debt and wound up $2.50 better off than he was before; and for the underpaid lawyer who helped to set two other men at peace with each other.

Another picture disputed by six cities, probably was taken by Roderick M. Cole of Peoria in 1858 during the time of the Lincoln-Douglas Debates. *Courtesy of the Illinois State Historical Library, Old State Capitol, Springfield, Illinois.*

Quotations on Work

Abraham Lincoln was born on a farm and reared to do farm work. Later in life he stated that his father taught him how to work hard, but he added that his father never taught him to like it. Young Lincoln admitted that he did not like farming. He much preferred to talk, laugh, read, tell stories, and crack jokes. Anything but farm work. But that did not mean that young Abe Lincoln was lazy. As a young man in his teens he was well-known as a hard worker, and for at least half of every year between his ages of fourteen and twenty-one his father hired him out to neighbors. Before the Thomas Lincoln family left Indiana to move to Illinois, young Lincoln was known as the best railsplitter in his part of Indiana.

In Illinois at the age of twenty-one, when he left his father's house, he still knew only farming. But he chose not to split rails and do manual labor for the rest of his life. He possessed the qualities of intelligence, ambition, and diligence which enabled him to overcome the handicaps of his humble birth.

Abraham Lincoln's total schooling amounted to less than one full year at public "blab schools" in Kentucky and Indiana. His training as a lawyer was a matter of independent study without the benefit of any other lawyer as a teacher and without ever having attended any law school or college. By reason of hard study and diligence, he became one of the most successful and respected lawyers in Illinois during his time.

In preparing his notes for a law lecture to the young lawyers in Springfield in 1850, Mr. Lincoln wrote the following:

The leading role for the lawyer, as for the man of every other calling, is diligence. Leave nothing for tomorrow which can be done today. Never let your correspondence fall behind. Whatever piece of business you have in hand, before stopping, do all the labor pertaining to it which can then be done. . . .

In those same notes for a law lecture, dated July 1, 1850, Lincoln wrote that skill in extemporaneous speaking should be practiced and cultivated by every lawyer. But emphatically he added:

. . . . there is not a more fatal error to young lawyers than relying too much on speech-making. If anyone, upon his rare powers of speaking, shall claim an exemption from the drudgery of the law, his case is a failure in advance.

When Isham Reavis, a young law student in 1855, wrote to Mr. Lincoln asking permission to study law under Lincoln's direction, the famous lawyer's answer included this statement:

I am from home too much of my time for a young man to read law with me advantageously. If you are resolutely determined to make a lawyer of yourself, the thing is more than half done already. It is but a small matter whether you read with anybody or not. I did not read with anyone. Get the books and read and study them till you understand them in their principles; that is the main thing. It is of no consequence to be in a large town while you are reading. I read at New Salem, which never had 300 people living in it. The books and your capacity for understanding them are just the same in all places.

On September 25, 1860, in writing to J. M. Brockman, who had written to ask about "the best mode of obtaining a thorough knowledge of the law," Lincoln stated:

The mode is very simple, though laborious and tedious. It is only to get the books, and read and study them carefully. Work, work, work, is the main thing. Yours truly, A. Lincoln.

While Mr. Lincoln was living in Washington, D.C. as a U.S. congressman from Illinois, he received a joint letter from his father and from his stepbrother, John D. Johnston. His father asked for $20 to save his land from sale. His stepbrother, who had requested and received from Lincoln several small amounts of money on previous occasions, asked for $80 for which he would almost give his "place in Heaven." Johnston had written the letter for his stepfather, and then added his own message requesting money for himself.

In answering the joint letter, Lincoln wrote on December 24, 1848, that he was pleased to send the requested $20 to his father but that he decided not to send $80 immediately to Johnston. This joint answer to a joint request is particularly interesting to Lincoln scholars today for revealing Lincoln's views on the subject of work and diligence. To his father he wrote: "I very cheerfully send you the twenty dollars, which sum you say is necessary to save your land from sale." To his step brother, Lincoln wrote:

Dear Johnston: Your request for eighty dollars I do not think it best to comply with now. At the various times when I have helped you a little, you have said to me, "We can get along very well now" but in a very short time I find you in the same difficulty again. Now this can happen only by some defect in your conduct. What that defect is, I think I know. You are not lazy, and still you are an idler. I doubt whether since I saw you, you have done a good whole day's work in any one day. You do not very much dislike to work; and still you do not work much, merely because it does not seem to you that you could get much for it. This habit of uselessly wasting time is the whole difficulty; and it is vastly important to you, and still more so to your children that you should break this habit. It is more important to them, because they have long to live, and can keep out of an idle habit before they are in it; easier than they can get out after they are in.

If the first part of Lincoln's answer to his step-brother's request seemed harsh and heartless, the remainder of the letter was truly loving and charitable. He wrote:

You are now in need of some ready money; and what I propose is that you shall go to work "tooth and nails" for somebody who will give you money for it. Let father and your boys take charge of things at home—prepare a crop, and make the crop; and you to go to work for the best money wages, or in discharge of any debt you owe, that you can get. And to secure for you a fair reward for your labor, I now promise you, that for every dollar you will, between this (date) and the first of next May, get for your own labor, either in money, or in your own indebtedness, I will then give you one other dollar.

Lincoln amplified on his offer by spelling out some conditions under which he would match Johnston's earnings dollar for dollar.

By this, if you hire yourself at ten dollars a month, from me you will get ten more, making twenty dollars a month for your work. In this, I do not mean you shall go off to St. Louis, or to the lead mines, or to the gold mines in California, but I mean for you to go at it for the best wages you can get close to home in Coles County. Now if you will do this, you will soon be out of debt, and what is better, you will have a habit that will keep you from getting in debt again. But if I should now clear you out, next year you will be just as deep in as ever. You say you would almost give your place in Heaven for $70 or $80. Then you value your place in Heaven very cheaply for I am sure you can with the offer I make you get the seventy or eighty dollars for four or five months work. You say if I

furnish you the money you will deed me the land, and, if you don't pay the money back, you will deliver possession. Nonsense! If you can't now live with the land, how will you then live without it? You have always been kind to me, and I do not now mean to be unkind to you. On the contrary, if you will but follow my advice, you will find it worth more than eight times eighty dollars to you. Affectionately, Your brother—A. Lincoln.

During the Civil War, President Lincoln had trouble getting his generals to function in their commands. General McClellan was a good organizer but he enjoyed basking in the glory of his generalship, and very reluctantly would he lead his troops into battle. Many of Lincoln's letters to his generals stressed the need for harder work and diligence in their commands. For example, an often quoted admonition written by Lincoln to Major General David Hunter, December 31, 1861, included the following statement:

"Act well your part, there all the honor lies." He who does SOMETHING at the head of a regiment will eclipse him who does NOTHING at the head of a hundred.

Secretary of War Edwin M. Stanton was the hardest working member of Lincoln's cabinet. Often he worked sixteen to eighteen hours a day, seven days a week. He was extremely efficient. When he assumed his office during the second year of the war, he quickly established system and order out of chaos. Lincoln greatly admired Stanton's hard work and diligence, even though he sometimes overrode

Stanton's commands for executions for dereliction of duty in the military. On one occasion Lincoln described Stanton as follows:

Stanton reminds me of an old Methodist preacher out West who became so energetic in the pulpit that his parishoners talked of putting rocks in his pockets to hold him down. Now we may be obliged to serve Stanton in the same way, but I guess we'll let him jump a while first.

Without Lincoln's quality of diligence, all of his other attributes of integrity, intellect, and idealism would have faded into darkness. As an intellectual, Lincoln preferred to do "intellectual work" than manual labor. And yet he had a high regard for manual labor, especially when a person labored diligently to improve his condition in life. In preparing for a speech on free labor, Lincoln wrote some notes on September 17, 1859, including the following comment:

There is no permanent class of hired laborers amongst us. Twenty-five years ago I was a hired laborer. The hired laborer of yesterday labors on his own account today, and will hire others to labor for him tomorrow.

Although Mr. Lincoln held very high regard for labor and for the rights of laboring men, he did not endorse any laboring people to resort to violence or destruction to change their condition of employment. Such a position was expressed in his message of March 21, 1864 to the New York Workingmen's Association.

Let not him who is houseless pull down the house of another, but let him labor diligently and build one for himself, thus by example assuring that his own shall be safe from violence when built.

Often called "the most famous of the beardless poses," this photograph of Lincoln was taken on the morning of February 27, 1860, in New York City by Mathew B. Brady, only a few hours before Lincoln delivered his Cooper Union Address. Lincoln reportedly said that this photograph and the Cooper Union Address together elected him to the Presidency.
Courtesy of the Illinois State Historical Library, Old State Capitol, Springfield, Illinois.

Quotations on Responsibility

The letters and speeches of Abraham Lincoln are filled with statements that reveal his strong sense of responsibility as an American citizen. Many of his most often quoted statements were expressions of personal and public responsibility for policies and programs that he urged be adopted for public good.

At the age of twenty-nine, when Lincoln was becoming recognized as a young lawyer of high ideals and bright political promise, he was invited to address the Young Men's Lyceum of Springfield, Illinois. For that occasion on January 27, 1838, the subject of his speech was The Perpetuation of Our Political Institutions. In denouncing the growth of mob law in some sections of the country, Lincoln asked: "How shall we fortify against it?" His answer was for all Americans to exercise their individual responsibilities as American citizens. As he stated:

Let every American, every lover of liberty, every well-wisher to his posterity, swear by the blood of the Revolution, never to violate in the least particular, the laws of the country; and never to tolerate their violation by others. As the patriots of '76 did to the support of the Declaration of Independence, so to the support of the Constitution and laws, let every American pledge his life, his property, and his sacred honor.

A strong epigramatical statement from that early public speech by Abraham Lincoln was:

Let every man remember that to violate the law is to trample on the blood of his father.

Lincoln's Cooper Union Address in New York City on February 27, 1860, paved the way for him to be nominated for president. That speech also produced several slogans which later rang like bells during ensuing political campaigns. Two of those slogans, which appealed to the sense of personal responsibility and duty by all citizens, were:

Neither let us be slandered from our duty by false accusations against us, nor frightened from it by menaces of destruction to the Government nor of dungeons to ourselves.

The most often quoted excerpt from the Cooper Union Address is:

Let us have faith that right makes might, and in that faith, let us, to the end, dare to do our duty as we understand it.

Following his election to the presidency, Lincoln was full aware of the tremendous responsibility he faced, as shown by the following statement in his Springfield, Farewell Address, February 11, 1861:

I now leave, not knowing when, or whether ever, I may return, with a task before me greater than that which rested upon Washington.

During the Civil War, President Lincoln was frequently reminded of his responsibility by various senators who tried to promote policies and decisions with which the president did not agree.

Prior to Edwin M. Stanton's appointment by Lincoln as secretary of war, the office had been filled by Simon Cameron of Pennsylvania. Partly because of graft and corruption in the war department under Cameron during 1861, and partly because of Union defeats at Bull Run and Ball's Bluff, public clamor demanded that Cameron be replaced. On January 12, 1862, the president appointed Cameron as minister to the Russian Court at St. Petersburg, and appointed Stanton as secretary of war.

Many of the Republican senators were not satisfied with the removal of only one cabinet member. They wanted all seven cabinet members replaced. A delegation of senators presented that proposal to the president. After listening to their arguments with courtesy, President Lincoln smiled and told the following story:

Gentlemen, your request for a change of the whole Cabinet because I have made one change, reminds me of a story I once heard out in Illinois. A farmer was very much troubled by skunks getting into his chicken coop. His wife insisted on his getting rid of them. One moonlight night he loaded his shotgun and waited for developments. After a while the wife heard the shotgun go off, and in a few minutes the farmer entered the house. "What luck did you have?" the wife asked. The farmer answered: "I hid myself behind the woodpile, with the shotgun pointed toward the hen roost, and before long there appeared not one skunk, but seven. I took aim, blazed away, and killed one, but he raised such a fearful smell that I concluded it was best to let the other six go."

The senators laughed heartily, saw the point of the story clearly, and realized that they had intruded upon a responsibility that the president fully understood.

General Grant, despite his reputation as a hard-drinking man, was also a hard-fighting general. He won battles. His victories at Vicksburg and in Tennessee prompted President Lincoln to place him in command of all armies in the East for the final push on Richmond. Other generals had procrastinated and basked in the glory of their command while calling for more men and supplies while they paraded in pompous self-admiration. When Lincoln met with Grant, he was determined to get the message across that Grant was not to act like a prima donna admiring himself with an ever-growing army as some had done. Rather than being blunt, Lincoln put his message in the form of a story which he related as follows:

At one time there was a great war among animals, and one side had great difficulty in getting a commander who had sufficient confidence in himself. Finally they found a monkey by the name of Jocko who said he thought he could command their army if his tail could be made a little longer. So they got more tail and spliced it on to his caudal appendage.

He looked at it admiringly, and then he said he thought he ought to have still more tail. The splicing process was repeated many times until they had coiled Jocko's tail around the room, filling all the space.

Still he called for more tail, and, there being no other place to coil it, they began wrapping it around his shoulders. He continued his call for more, and they kept winding the additional tail around him until its weight broke him down.

General Grant quickly saw the meaning of the president's story and assured him that he would get on with the campaign at once.

President Lincoln understood that a personal responsibility must be based in part upon an appreciation of both esthetic and material values. In major speeches like the Gettysburg Address and the Second Inaugural Address, he prefaced his appeals to responsibility with a review of values which Americans held sacred.

Among the hundreds of Lincoln's letters, proclamations, and minor speeches which have received little or no public attention, many are strikingly beautiful. One such communication, expressing great depth of appreciation for God, man, and nature, is Lincoln's Proclamation of Thanksgiving, October 3, 1863, quoted here in part, and in a form that reveals the quality of poetry:

The year that is drawing toward its close
has been filled with the blessings
of fruitful fields and healthful skies.
These bounties are so constantly enjoyed
that we are prone to forget
the source from which they come.
They are the gracious gifts of the Most High God.
It has seemed to me, ... that they should be
solemnly, reverently, and gratefully
acknowledged as with one heart and one voice
by the whole American people.

The poetical beauty in Lincoln's thinking and speaking was revealed most clearly in his plea for reconstruction with amnesty in the final paragraph of the Second Inaugural Address, delivered on March 4, 1865.

With malice toward none:
with Charity for all;
With firmness in the right,
as God gives us to see the right;
Let us strive on
to finish the work we are in;
to bind up the nation's wounds;
to care for him who shall have borne the battle,
and for his widow, and his orphans;
to do all which may achieve and cherish
a just and a lasting peace,
Among ourselves, and with all nations.

In 1976, the responsibility still remained with the American people for finishing the work which Lincoln prescribed in his Second Inaugural Address.

Shortly after the nomination by his party for the Presidency, this photograph was taken by Alexander Hesler in Springfield, June 3, 1860. Of this photograph Lincoln reportedly said: "That looks better and expresses me better than any I have ever seen; if it pleases the people, I am satisfied." *Courtesy of the Illinois State Historical Library, Old State Capitol, Springfield, Illinois.*

Quotations on Logical Thinking

As a self-educated country lawyer, how was Abraham Lincoln able to cope intellectually with such brilliant men as Senator Charles Sumner, Congressman Thaddeus Stevens, and Editor Horace Greeley?

What special qualities of mind enabled Lincoln to resolve the problems of slavery, freedom, emancipation, amnesty, and the readmission of Southern States into the Union?

What particular mental abilities guided Lincoln in composing the wisdom of his Gettysburg Address and his Second Inaugural?

Answers to these questions might be found by analyzing the major qualities of Lincoln's intellect under five headings—premises, evidence, reasoning, imagery, and beauty.

Mr. Lincoln admitted that he always thought slowly and carefully on a subject before making up his mind. The following quotation by Lincoln testifies to his process of thinking.

Among my earliest recollections, I remember how, when a mere child, I used to get irritated when anybody talked to me in a way I could not understand. I can remember going to my little bedroom, after hearing the neighbors talk of an evening with my father, and spending no small part of the night . . . . trying to make out what was the exact meaning of some of their, to me, dark sayings. . . . I was not satisfied until I had put it in language plain enough, as I thought, for any boy I knew to comprehend. This was a kind of passion with me . . . .

I am never easy now, when I am handling a thought, till I have bounded it north, and bounded it east, bounded it south, and bounded it west.

The following testimonial, on Lincoln's mental processes, was made by William Herndon, Lincoln's law partner in Springfield.

Lincoln's perceptions were slow, cold, clear and exact. Everything came to him in its precise shape and color. No lurking illusion or other error, false in itself and clad for the moment in robes of splendor, ever passed undetected over the threshold of his mind. He saw all things through a perfect mental lens. There was no diffraction or refraction.

Premises in Lincoln's Thinking

Underlying the thinking process of every person are basic assumptions, philosophical beliefs, called premises. All available evidence and logical reasoning mean nothing in a controversy if the basic premise underlying the argument is not agreed upon by the participants. In all of his discussions on the problem of slavery, Mr. Lincoln was explicit in stating the basic premises from which he argued.

When Mr. Lincoln emerged from political retirement in 1854 following the passage of the Kansas-Nebraska Act, which repealed the Missouri Compromise and adopted a policy of popular sovereignty, he immediately emphasized the wrongness of the premises behind that doctrine. As he stated in his speech at Peoria, October 16, 1854:

I think that it (the repeal of the Missouri Compromise) is wrong; wrong in its direct effect, letting slavery into Kansas and Nebraska; and wrong in its prospective principle, allowing it to spread.

In the same speech at Peoria, in answer to what Senator Douglas had said the day before in the same city, Lincoln declared:

. . . . whether it (the doctrine of self-government) has such just application depends upon whether the negro IS NOT or IS a man. If he IS NOT a man, in that case, he who IS a man may, as a matter of self-government, do just as he pleases with him. But if the negro IS a man, is it not to that extent a total destruction of self-government to say that he too shall not govern HIMSELF?

Lincoln hammered away at this same major theme during all of his political speaking from that time, 1854, until his election to the presidency. In the vital Lincoln-Douglas Debates of 1858, he repeatedly emphasized the importance of the basic premise which anyone assumed toward slavery. At the sixth debate at Quincy, Illinois, on October 13, 1858, he stated:

I suggest that the difference of opinion, reduced to its terms, is no other than the difference between the men who think slavery a wrong, and those who do not think it a wrong. We also oppose it as an evil so far as it seeks to spread itself.

On October 15, 1858, in the seventh and final debate with Douglas, Lincoln reiterated his position as follows:

The real issue in this controversy—the one pressing on every mind—is the sentiment on the part of one class that looks upon the institution of slavery as a wrong, and of another class that does not look upon it as a wrong.

In his Cooper Union Institute speech in New York City on February 27, 1860, Mr. Lincoln stated the following:

If slavery is right, all words, acts, laws and constitutions against it are themselves wrong, and should be silenced and swept away. If it is right, we cannot justly object to its nationality—its universality; if it is wrong, they cannot justly insist upon its extension—its enlargement.

As Lincoln emphasized, the simple difference between the thinking of proslavery and antislavery advocates was a matter of premises, or basic assumptions, regarding the moral aspect of slavery.

When Congress passed the harsh Wade-Davis Bill which set up Congressional "conditions" for a state to rejoin the Union, Lincoln vetoed the bill for two main reasons: Lincoln denied that Congress could abolish slavery if it was authorized in a state constitution. Such an action, Lincoln declared, would require an amendment to the United States Constitution. Also, the Congressional conditions for a state rejoining the Union could possibly include punishments and thus would prolong the conflict and increase the bitterness between North and South. Lincoln's basic position was: reconstruction with amnesty.

A delegation of senators (Charles Sumner, George Boutwell, and Zachariah Chandler) came to Lincoln to pressure the president to sign the Wade-Davis Bill, and to remind him that Congressional authority should replace executive action on the readmission of states into the Union. To the assembled senators on July 4, 1864, President Lincoln replied:

I conceive that I may in an emergency do things on military grounds which cannot be done constitutionally by Congress.

After the senators had departed, Lincoln stated to his cabinet:

This bill and the position of these gentlemen seem to me, in asserting that the insurrectionary States are no longer in the Union, to make the fatal admission that States, whenever they please, may of their own motion dissolve their connection with the Union. Now we cannot survive that admission.

Here again, Lincoln had refuted the premise upon which his opponents based their argument.

Use of Evidence in Lincoln's Thinking

In his debates with Senator Douglas, Abraham Lincoln gained strong advantage by basing his arguments on sound and true evidence. In the first debate at Ottawa, Douglas asserted that Lincoln and Judge Trumbull had conspired to destroy the old Whig Party and the Democratic Party to form the new Republican Party. Both Lincoln and Trumbull denied the charge, and Douglas was never able to prove his accusation.

During the first debate at Ottawa, Douglas read a set of resolutions which he claimed were passed at the first Republican State Convention in 1854, and which he claimed were voted for by Lincoln at the Convention. Lincoln responded:

As to those resolutions that he (Douglas) took such length of time to read, as being the platform of the Republican Party in 1854, I say I never had anything to do with them. . . . It is also true that I went away from Springfield, when the convention was in session, to attend court in Tazwell County.

Somehow, Douglas had mistakenly quoted from a wrong set of resolutions, and had only assumed that Lincoln was present at the convention. His carelessness about his facts became embarrassing. The *Chicago Press and Tribune* exposed the so-called fraud before the second debate was held at Freeport where Lincoln commented:

It turns out that those resolutions were never passed at any convention or public meeting that I had any part in. Now it turns out that he had got hold of some resolutions passed at some convention or public meeting in Kane County.

In the Freeport and Jonesboro debates, Douglas claimed, in support of his popular sovereignty doctrine, that slavery could not enter a new territory without police regulations. Lincoln refuted Douglas by showing historically that the institution of slavery was originally planted upon this continent without police regulations. Furthermore, he proved that Dred Scott had been taken into Minnesota Territory and held there in slavery without any police regulations to protect the institution of slavery.

Lincoln's greatest triumph involving the use of evidence was when he addressed the Cooper Union Institute in New York City, February 27, 1860. Instead of giving his usual speech for pointing out the contradiction between popular sovereignty and the Dred Scott decision, Lincoln chose to refute a claim which Senator Douglas had made in a speech in Ohio, namely; that the framers of the Constitution intended that the federal government should have no authority to control slavery in the territories. From his lengthy researches in the Illinois State Library, Lincoln proved that a strong majority of the signers of the Constitution held no such opinion as Douglas

had asserted. As Lincoln summarized his findings:

They (our founding fathers) certainly understood that no proper division of local from Federal authority, nor any part of the Constitution, forbade the Federal Government to control slavery in the Federal Territories.

Lincoln further challenged anybody to prove that even one of the seventy-six members of the Congress which passed the first ten amendments to the Constitution ever held the view which Douglas claimed. So carefully prepared was Lincoln's Cooper Union Address, and so accurate was Lincoln in his use of evidence, that historians generally agree that this particular speech gained for Lincoln the nomination of his party for the presidency.

Formal Logic in Lincoln's Thinking

Lincoln's knowledge and use of formal logic was much more academic than many of his contemporaries ever suspected. In the field of deductive reasoning, he was fully aware of the three elements upon which valid deductions rest (premises + evidence + logical inference = valid conclusion). After clarifying his premises, and after establishing the truth of his evidence, he proceeded to apply the tests of logical inference as carefully as a classroom professor of logic.

In his rough and tumble debating with Senator Douglas, Lincoln sometimes became extremely academic by referring technically to the component parts of his arguments. He even used the word "syllogistic" in the Galesburg debate, October 7,

1858, when he took the various assertions of Senator Douglas and arranged them as a formal syllogism. As Lincoln argued:

Now, remembering the provision of the Constitution which I have read, affirming that that instrument is the supreme law of the land; that the Judges of every State shall be bound by it, any law or Constitution of any state to the contrary notwithstanding; that the right of property in a slave is affirmed in that Constitution, is made, formed into and cannot be separated from it without breaking it; durable as the instrument; part of the instrument:— what follows as a short and even syllogistic argument from it? I think it follows, and I submit to the consideration of men capable of arguing, whether as I state it in syllogistic form the argument has any fault in it:

Nothing in the Constitution or laws of any State can destroy a right distinctly and expressly affirmed in the Constitution of the United States:

The right of property in a slave is distinctly and expressly affirmed in the Constitution of the United States;

Therefore, nothing in the Constitution or laws of any State can destroy the right of property in a slave.

Continuing his explanation, Lincoln stated:

I believe that no fault can be pointed out in that argument; assuming the truth of the premises, the conclusion, so far as I have the capacity to understand it, follows inevitably. There is a fault in it as I think, but the fault is not in the reasoning; the falsehood in fact is a fault of the premises. I believe that the right of property in a slave IS NOT distinctly and expressly affirmed in the Constitution, and Judge Douglas thinks it IS.

In Springfield, Illinois, on June 26, 1857, speaking in response to Senator Douglas's defense of the Dred Scott decision, Lincoln exposed what logicians would call the fallacy of alternatives not exhaustive in a disjunctive syllogism.

He (Douglas) finds the Republicans insisting that the Declaration of Independence includes all men, black as well as white; and forthwith he boldly denies it includes negroes at all, and proceeds to argue gravely that all who contend it does, do so only because they want to vote, and marry with negroes.

Now I protest against this counterfeit logic which concludes that because I do not want a black woman for a slave I must necessarily want her for a wife. I need not have her for either; I can just leave her alone.

During the fifth Lincoln-Douglas debate at Galesburg, October 7, 1858, Lincoln reasoned:

Judge Douglas declared if people of any community want slavery, they have a right to have it. He can say that logically, if he says that there is no wrong in slavery; but if you admit that there is a wrong in it, he cannot logically say that anybody has a right to do wrong.

Throughout his political career, Lincoln's exposure of fallacies in the arguments of his opponents suggests that his intellectual powers were equal to, if not far superior to, the mental abilities of the men who opposed him.

Telling a story was an important way that Lincoln used for persuading a listener. To Lincoln a story became a labor-saving device. Frequently when discussion on any topic began to bog down in broad assertions and generalities, Lincoln would interrupt by saying, "That reminds me of a story."

Lincoln thoroughly understood the importance of taking ideas out of the realm of abstractions and generalities. He knew that people think most easily when visual images are created for them. He is reported to have spoken to Chauncey M. Depew, noted American lawyer and after-dinner speaker, in the following manner:

> *They say I tell a great many stories; I reckon I do, but I have found in the course of a long experience that common people—common people—take them as they run, are more easily influenced and informed through the medium of a broad illustration than in any other way.*

Source materials for Lincoln's stories came largely from his own experiences during his earlier life in Illinois. However, he did enjoy reading the writings of the humorists of his day, and occasionally he would borrow a story from Joe Miller's Joke Book, or from the satirical writings on politics by Petroleum V. Nasby.

In public debates and discussions, as well as during legal cases in court, Lincoln often had to oppose speakers who employed all of the high-powered oratory and bombast that they could muster to serve their cause. On such occasions Lincoln, with his folksy, conversational manner, would seem to be inferior. But sometimes, when Lincoln felt certain that his opponent was overdoing the oratorical manner, he would make a humorous comment as:

> *He can compress the most words into the fewest ideas of any man in Illinois.*

On one evening during a speech that he was delivering, Lincoln was frequently interrupted by a noisy, quarrelsome man who asked long questions which he answered himself with long-winded answers which were very much off the point. Good-naturedly, Lincoln tolerated those interruptions longer than he should have. Knowing that his audience was somewhat annoyed by the noisy detractor, Lincoln decided to tell the following story about a steamboat and let the story and its effect on the audience decide the fate of the interrupter.

> *My boisterous friend reminds me of a certain little steamboat that used to bustle and puff and wheeze about on the Ohio River. It had a five foot boiler and a seven foot whistle. Biggest and prettiest whistle on any boat on the entire river. But every time they blew that big whistle it used all of the steam in the boiler and the boat just stopped. That's the way it is with my friend. Every time he opens his mouth the discussion comes to a stop.*

As Lincoln finished his story, the audience howled with laughter. The "boisterous friend" made no further interruptions.

Using figurative analogies, which have minimal argumentative value but which possess strong visual imagery for persuasive effect, was a frequent technique of Lincoln in all kinds of communications.

One day while he was riding on a passenger train he was discussing his position on the issue of slavery and the question of letting slavery spread into new territories. He explained that while he looked upon slavery as evil, he believed that it could not be immediately destroyed where it was accepted in the

Southern states. At the same time, it must not be allowed to spread for fear of destroying the nation. Lincoln's companion could not easily accept what he believed was Lincoln's contradictory position on the issue. Then Lincoln noticed that sitting in a seat somewhat ahead of them was a man who had a large and ugly wen on the back of his neck. Calling his companion's attention to the wen, Lincoln explained:

Slavery is somewhat like the wen that you see on the back of that man's neck. If it were cut off immediately without the necessary precautions, the man could easily bleed to death. However, if it were allowed to grow unattended and without any kind of careful medical surgery, it could easily spread until it would completely disfigure or incapacitate the man. As the man must submit to carefully planned surgery to save his life from being destroyed by the wen, so must the nation carefully and tolerantly treat the problem of slavery in a way so as not to destroy the Union.

On the matter of how the border states would react to a presidential proclamation emancipating the slaves within their borders, President Lincoln was extremely sensitive. Of the four states—Delaware, Maryland, Kentucky and Missouri—perhaps all of them would leave the Union if his proposed proclamation included them. If they should secede from the Union, not enough states would remain in the Union to make legislation by Congress constitutional. Also, including them in his proclamation would essentially stop all support which the Union was receiving from them. Accordingly, on several occasions, to strengthen people's understanding of his position, Lincoln told a story which ran something like this:

One morning a farmer looked into the bedroom where his two young sons were sleeping. To his horror he saw that a large black snake had curled itself up and was sleeping peacefully on the bed between the two boys. The farmer's first impulse was to grab an ax or a shotgun and try to kill the snake. But on second thought, he knew that he ran the risk of injuring his sons if he tried to kill the snake. And so he devised a plan of enticing the snake out of the bed. In a similar manner the institution of slavery in the border states must not be disturbed until it can be enticed to leave without destroying the states that are still members of the family of states in the Union.

Whenever Lincoln told that story his listeners seemed to offer little or no refutation. His use of imagery in this case was more effective than all of his arguments based upon the Constitution.

Early in 1863, President Lincoln appointed General Joseph Hooker to replace General Ambrose Burnside as commander of the Union Army of the Potomac. Following the disastrous Battle of Chancellorsville, General Hooker took up defenses near Fredericksburg. But Confederate General Robert E. Lee began to move his army westward from Fredericksburg in preparation for invading the North a second time. General Hooker delayed following Lee until he almost got caught with his army in an awkward position. Sensing Hooker's possible predicament, Lincoln wrote the following suggestions regarding possible military strategy:

I have but one idea which I think worth suggesting to you, and that is in case you find Lee coming to the North of the Rappahannock, I would by no means cross to the South of it.

In one word, I would not take any risk of being entangled upon the river, like an ox jumped half over a fence, and liable to be torn by dogs, front and rear, without a fair chance to gore one way or kick the other.

Stories have been told by the score of President Lincoln's heart rending sympathy for wives and mothers who came to him pleading that their husbands or sons not be executed for falling asleep on duty or from deserting during battle. Lincoln refused to grant reprieves to "bounty hunters," volunteers who collected bounties of $200 or $300 for joining the army, and then deserted before entering battle. But he was always willing to review a case when he felt that execution was too harsh a penalty on the soldier, or when it would cause extreme hardship to the soldier's family.

One day, following an extremely emotional plea by a woman for her husband who was sentenced for execution, President Lincoln signed the order for reprieve, and then said to his attorney general:

Speed, die when I may, I want it said of me by those who know me best,—that I have always plucked a thistle and planted a flower whenever I thought a flower would grow.

Beauty in Lincoln's Thinking

Edwin M. Stanton, who became Lincoln's secretary of war, once referred to the president as "the original Illinois gorilla." Other associates of Lincoln, on meeting him for the first time, were disappointed by his homely appearance and ungraceful movements. Yet Stanton, and others who came to know him well, eventually overlooked his outward unattractiveness, and praised him for his inward beauty.

Lincoln's two personal secretaries, John G. Nicolay and John Hay, wrote in their biography, *Abraham Lincoln, A History*, about the "inner man," his mind and soul and spirit as "that tender humanity and Christian charity in which he walked among his fellow countrymen."

When human thoughts and feelings are expressed in their clearest and purest form, they often emerge in a poetic style. When Mr. Lincoln accepted the nomination of his party to run against Stephen A. Douglas for the office of U.S. Senator, his speech on June 16, 1858 became known as the House Divided Speech. His opening sentence, often quoted by college and high school debaters, possessed a simplicity and rhythm which enables it to be written as poetry:

If we could first know where we are,
*   and whither we are tending,*
We could better judge what to do
*   and how to do it.*

The reason that this particular speech became known as the House Divided Speech was because he used a Biblical quotation as a slogan for the central thought of his speech. He declared (by quoting from the Bible):

A house divided against itself cannot stand.

Following his bombshell statement, he explained:

I believe this government cannot endure,
   permanently half slave and half free.
I do not expect the Union to be dissolved—
   I do not expect the house to fall—
But I do expect it will cease to be divided.
   It will become all one thing, or the other.

By the time that Mr. Lincoln had reached national prominence, his particular style often crystallized thoughts and feelings into the form of strong slogans and rhythmical verse. The House Divided Speech was concluded with the statement:

Wise councils may accelerate or mistakes delay it,
   But sooner or later the victory is sure to come.

The conclusion of the Cooper Union Address implored the people:

Let us have faith that right makes might,
   And in that faith, let us, to the end,
Dare to do our duty as we understand it.

Lincoln's Farewell Address at Springfield, Illinois, when he departed for Washington, D.C., ended with the words:

To His care commending you,
   As I hope in your prayers
You will commend me,
   I bid you an affectionate farewell.

A quotation from Lincoln's renowned Gettysburg Address has become the commonly used definition of American democracy: government of the people, by the people, for the people. Lincoln's Second Inaugural Address can be read easily as a poem instead of as a speech. The final paragraph of that message began with a beautiful epigrammatical summation of his executive policy of reconstruction with amnesty:

With malice toward none: with Charity for all.

This photograph was taken by Mathew Brady in Washington, D.C. on January 8, 1864. Many Lincoln scholars consider it the best portrait of Lincoln standing. *Courtesy of the Illinois State Historical Library, Old State Capitol, Springfield, Illinois.*

Quotations on Government

Representing Abraham Lincoln's opinions on government and politics, is his speech The Perpetuation of Our Political Institutions, delivered on January 27, 1838, to the Young Men's Lyceum of Springfield, Illinois. As a young lawyer and state legislator, at age twenty-nine, Mr. Lincoln made the following comment about American democracy and government:

We find ourselves under the government of a system of political institutions, conducing more essentially to the ends of civil and religious liberty, than any of which the history of former times tell us.

Immediately prior to that speech in 1838, a series of riots and public disorders had occurred in various parts of the country. All of them were related to public reactions to issues on slavery and abolitionism. Mr. Lincoln held his own private convictions on both issues, but above all partisan politics he placed a public regard for law and order as the first duty of every citizen. His apprehension was expressed in these words:

There is, even now, something of ill-omen amongst us. I mean the increasing disregard for law which pervades the country; the growing disposition to substitute the wild and furious passions, in lieu of the sober judgment of Courts.

In that day and age Lincoln believed that America could never be conquered by overseas armies. But he did express concern that our national security could be threatened by civil disorders.

If destruction be our lot, we must ourselves be its author and finisher. As a nation of freemen, we must live through all time, or die by suicide.

Throughout his career as a lawyer and statesman, Mr. Lincoln held the highest regard for the Constitution of the United States. Even when the national attention became focused upon the moral issue of slavery, Lincoln did not allow his own personal hatred of slavery to overrule the protection which the Constitution gave to slavery as an institution. He believed that slavery, unless the Constitution were amended, could legally be allowed in those states where state laws protected its practice.

The passage of the Kansas-Nebraska Act in 1854 specifically repealed the Compromise of 1820 and permitted the extension of slavery into new territories. Mr. Lincoln strongly opposed that act, which was authored by and promoted through Congress by Senator Stephen A. Douglas. However, in opposing the extension of slavery, he also insisted that existing slavery should be left alone. In his speech at Peoria on October 16, 1854, Lincoln acknowledged that slavery in the South was protected by the Constitution.

> *Before proceeding, let me say I think I have no prejudice against the Southern people. They are just what we would be in their situation. If slavery did not now exist amongst them, they would not introduce it. If it did now exist amongst us, we should not instantly give it up. This I believe of the masses north and south.*

> *When southern people tell us they are no more responsible for the origin of slavery than we, I acknowledge the fact. When it is said that the institution exists, and that it is very difficult to get rid of it, in any satisfactory way, I can understand and appreciate the saying.*

> *When they remind us of their constitutional rights, I acknowledge them, not grudgingly, but fully, and fairly.*

In a speech delivered at Edwardsville, Illinois, on May 18, 1858, Lincoln repeated his basic belief in self-government, his respect for the Constitution, and his opposition to the indefinite spread of slavery.

> *I, too, believe in self-government as I understand it; but I do not understand that the privilege one man takes of making a slave of another, or holding him as such, is any part of "self-government." To call it so is, to my mind, simply absurd and ridiculous. I am for the people of the whole nation doing just as they please in all matters which concern the whole nation; for those of each part doing just as they choose in all matters which concern no other part; and for each individual doing just as he chooses in all matters which concern nobody else. This is the principle. Of course I am content with any exception which the Constitution, or the actually existing state of things, makes a necessity. But neither the principle nor the exception will admit the indefinite spread and perpetuity of human slavery.*

As in his other debates with Senator Douglas, Abraham Lincoln at the sixth debate held at Quincy, Illinois on October 13, 1858, repeated his belief that the Constitution protected the institution of slavery in those states where it already existed:

> *I have no purpose directly or indirectly to interfere with the institution (slavery) in the States where it exists. I believe I have no right to do so.*

At the seventh and last debate with Douglas held

at Alton, Illinois, on October 15, 1858, Lincoln said:

I suppose most of us believe that the people of the Southern States are entitled to a Congressional fugitive slave law—that it is a right fixed in the Constitution. But it cannot be made available to them without Congressional legislation. And as the right is constitutional I agree that the legislation shall be granted to it. . . and that not that we like the institution of slavery. . . .Why then do I yield support to a fugitive slave law? Because I do not understand that the Constitution, which guarantees that right, can be supported without it.

At the time that Mr. Lincoln was elected president, he still believed that the Constitution gave protection to slavery in the Southern states, and he promised not to interfere with it where it existed. In his First Inaugural Address on March 4, 1861, President Lincoln stated:

I now reiterate these sentiments: . . . that the property, peace and security of no section are to be in anywise endangered by the now incoming Administration. I add, too, that all the protection which, consistently with the Constitution and the laws, can be given, will be cheerfully given to all the States when lawfully demanded, for whatever cause—as cheerfully to one section, as to another.

Toward the conclusion of his First Inaugural Address, President Lincoln declared his most solemn oath to defend the government.

In your hands, my dissatisfied countrymen, and not in mine, is the momentous issue of Civil War. The government will not assail you. You can have no conflict, without being yourselves the aggressors. You have no oath registered in Heaven to destroy the government, while I shall have the most solemn one to preserve, protect and defend it.

As the nation sank deeper into the agony of Civil War, President Lincoln found that his prime political policy was Preservation of the Union. In his message to Congress on December 3, 1861, the President declared:

The Union must be preserved, and hence all indispensable means must be employed. We should not be in haste to determine that radical and extreme measures, which may reach the loyal as well as the disloyal, are indispensable.

As the Civil War continued, the president was pressured to proclaim the emancipation of the slaves throughout the nation. Lincoln hesitated in doing so because he believed that slavery was constitutionally legal in the Southern states. Also, with Union armies unable to win any military victories, he knew that such a proclamation would carry no effectiveness at home, and would be scoffed at abroad. In his reply to an Emancipation Memorial Presented by Chicago Christians on September 13, 1862, the president stated:

What good would a proclamation of emancipation from me do, especially as we are now situated? I do not want to issue a document that the whole world will see must necessarily be inoperative,. . . .Would my word free the slaves, when I cannot even enforce the Constitution in the rebel States?

Then the president added his belief that as commander-in-chief of armed forces in time of war he possessed the authority to free the slaves as a war measure.

Understand, I raise no objections against it on legal or constitutional grounds; for as commander-in-chief of the army and navy, in time of war, I suppose I have a right to take any measure which may best subdue the enemy. I view the matter as a practical war measure, to be decided upon according to the advantages or disadvantages it may offer to the suppression of the rebellion.

Horace Greeley, publisher of the *New York Tribune*, had been a supporter of Lincoln during the early days of the Civil War. But by mid-summer of 1862, Greeley became exasperated with Lincoln's delay in emancipating the slaves. As an abolitionist, Greeley demanded through his newspaper that Lincoln should emancipate the slaves immediately, on moral grounds, without waiting for a military victory. On August 22, 1862, the president wrote to Greeley and allowed his letter to be published. The often-quoted portion of that letter stipulated clearly that whatever he did in relation to the black race would be done secondarily to his prime policy of saving the Union.

My paramount object in this struggle is to save the Union, and it is not either to save or to destroy slavery. If I could save the Union without freeing any slave I would do it; and if I could save the Union by freeing some and leaving others alone I would do that. What I do about slavery, and the colored race, I do because it helps to save the Union; and what I forbear, I forbear because I do not believe it helps to save the Union.

Eventually the president did exercise his power to emancipate the slaves. Shortly after the Union army victory at Antietam, he announced his intention to emancipate the slaves, beginning January 1, 1863, in those states and parts of states that remained in rebellion against the Union. On moral grounds he claimed clear authority for so doing. On constitutional grounds he claimed that the authority to do so was fully within his power and duty, as commander-in-chief in time of war, to help to defeat the enemy. As proclaimed by President Lincoln on January 1, 1863:

And by virtue of the power, and for the purpose aforesaid, I do order and declare that all persons held as slaves within said designated States, and parts of States, are, and henceforward shall be free.
And upon this act, sincerely believed to be an act of justice, warranted by the Constitution, upon military necessity, I invoke the considerate judgment of mankind, and the gracious favor of Almighty God.

By that proclamation, Lincoln did not free the slaves in the border states or in those parts of Southern states that were not in rebellion against the Union. He believed that he had no Constitutional right to do so. But he did propose the Thirteenth Amendment of the U.S. Constitution, which freed all slaves in all states, which passed in Congress, and which he signed as president, but which was not ratified by enough state legislatures until after his death.

One use of his presidential authority for preserving the Union, for which Lincoln was severely criticized, was his suspension of the writ of habeas corpus following the severe draft riots in New York City during the summer of 1863.

During the Civil War, the pacifists in the North were called Copperheads. Some of them were Southern sympathizers, and some were merely against warfare on moral grounds. All of them were opposed to the drafting of men for service in the Union armed forces. Often they showed their resentment by barn burning and harassment of recruiting officers.

The two great Union victories on July 4, 1863, at Gettysburg and Vicksburg, were won at a tremendous cost in men, killed and wounded. Of necessity the next draft called for higher quotas of men from all states for August. Copperhead riots developed in Ohio, Indiana, Pennsylvania, Wisconsin, Illinois, and in New York City where mobs overran an armory and used the stolen guns to fight the police in the streets. Civil authorities were unable to quell the fighting. For three days the rioters barricaded some streets, burned and pillaged buildings and killed scores of blacks. Altogether about 1,000 people were killed in the riot.

Because the rioters had revolted against the national authority in time of war, and because civil authorities were unable to handle the problem, President Lincoln used his war-time powers to suspend the writ of habeas corpus and to decree that the rioters should be tried in military courts instead of in civilian courts where some sympathetic judges were dismissing the charges against them. In the military courts, the draft resisters and rioters received trials without delay. The justice portioned out was severe. In civilian courts the trials had dragged out at great length and expense. Oddly enough, Lincoln's suspension of the writ of habeas

corpus ended the draft riots immediately. And the quotas for August 1863 were filled quickly.

By some standards, President Lincoln acted like a dictator. He expanded the army, he spent money not yet appropriated by Congress, he drafted men into military service, and he suspended the writ of habeas corpus—temporarily. Why? For a man who believed implicitly in the Constitution and in the basic freedoms of the people, his actions indeed reflected a dictator.

Abraham Lincoln himself gave the best defense for those actions which appeared dictatorial. In a letter of April 4, 1864, to Albert G. Hodges, editor of the Frankfort, Kentucky *Commonwealth*, the President explained in writing, as requested by Mr. Hodges, what the two men had discussed several days earlier. Excerpts from that letter include:

My oath to preserve the Constitution to the best of my ability, imposed upon me the duty of preserving, by every indispensable means, that government— that nation—of which that Constitution was the organic law.

Was it possible to lose the nation, and yet preserve the Constitution? By general law, life and limb must be protected; yet often a limb must be amputated to save a life; but a life is never wisely given to save a limb.

I felt that measures, otherwise unconstitutional, might become lawful, by becoming indispensable to the preservation of the Constitution, through the preservation of the nation. Right or wrong, I assumed this ground, and now avow it. I could not feel that, to the best of my ability, I had even tried to preserve the Constitution, if, to save slavery, or any minor matter, I should permit the wreck of government, country, and Constitution all together.

Earlier in his administration, Lincoln applied the above principle by forbidding General Fremont's attempted military emancipation of slaves in Missouri, by objecting to Secretary of War Cameron's arming of black soldiers, and by forbidding General Hunter's attempted military emancipation of slaves in certain parts of the South.

Originally, Lincoln did not believe that the indispensable necessity had yet arrived. Yet he himself eventually authorized all three of those actions under the reason of indispensable necessity. His ending of the letter to Hodges reflects the true greatness of his thinking and feeling toward humanity, God, and his fellow countrymen.

I claim not to have controlled events, but confess plainly that events have controlled me. Now at the end of three years' struggle the nation's condition is not what either party, or any man devised, or expected. God alone can claim it. Whither it is tending seems plain. If God now wills the removal of a great wrong, and wills also that we of the North as well as you of the South, shall pay fairly for our complicity in that wrong, impartial history will find therein new cause to attest and revere the justice and goodness of God. Yours truly, A. Lincoln.

Historians generally agree that Lincoln saved the Union and freed the slaves. But the order of those two achievements was important. First, the Union had to be saved. Dictatorial actions which he seemed to follow were only temporary. None of his war-time powers became permanent. All of them were relinquished at or before the end of the war. And in the celebrated Milligan Case, the U.S. Supreme Court ruled in 1866 that Lincoln's use of military courts to try civilian rioters against the draft was wrong. But by 1866 both Lincoln and the Civil War were dead. And yet, without Lincoln's temporary suspension of the writ of habeas corpus, the North itself might have been torn to shreds, the South might have become independent, and the Union might have been lost.

Lincoln's theory and practice of government will always stand out in the conscience of men by his plea at Gettysburg, November 19, 1863:

. . . . that government of the people, by the people, for the people, shall not perish from the earth.

On January 8, 1864, in Washington, D.C., Mathew Brady took this photograph of Lincoln sitting. *Courtesy of the Illinois State Historical Library, Old State Capitol, Springfield, Illinois.*

Quotations on Economic Enterprise

Abraham Lincoln was not an academic economist. However, during his career as a lawyer, as a congressman, and as president, he developed a basic philosophy of economics. That philosophy also grew out of his early experiences as a farm laborer, flat boatman, surveyor, storekeeper, postmaster, and self-taught lawyer.

During his early manhood, Abraham Lincoln learned the value of hard work and meticulous attention to details of his trades. As a railsplitter he gained recognition not only for the volume of rails that he could produce in one day but also for the excellence of their size and uniformity. That took hard work. As a surveyor he mastered the basics and application of geometry and trigonometry to the art of measuring land. That took hard study. Indepen-

dent study. No schools to attend. He was born into relative poverty, but he chose not to remain in poverty. As a lawyer he gradually acquired a degree of wealth, even by charging small fees to his clients. By the time that he was elected president, Mr. Lincoln was comfortably well-off. His economic philosophy, developed during his formative years, and followed throughout his adult career, was basically a laissez-faire, free enterprise system. Lincoln's theory of political economy was based upon three premises:

1. Self-interest, including a desire for material gain, motivates the work habits of most people.

2. Competition, among laborers and producers, promotes progress.

3. The three sources of economic production

(land, labor, capital) each deserve equal protection by government without a weakening of the rights of the other two—or stated otherwise—

Government should neither help nor hinder each of the sources of economic production (land, labor, capital) at the expense of the rights of the other two.

Self-interest: In his belief that self-interest, including a desire for material gain, motivates work habits, Mr. Lincoln made numerous statements. For example, regarding himself, he said:

Every man is said to have his peculiar ambition. Whether it be true or not, I can say, for one, that I have no other so great as that of being truly esteemed by my fellow man, by rendering myself worthy of their esteem.

In a speech that Mr. Lincoln made on March 6, 1860, at New Haven, Connecticut, following his greatly successful Cooper Union Institute Address in New York City, he stated:

What is the true condition of the laborer? I take it that it is best for all to leave each man free to acquire property as fast as he can. Some will get wealthy. I don't believe in a law to prevent a man from getting rich; it would do more harm than good. So while we do not propose any war upon capital, we do wish to allow the humblest man an equal chance to get rich with everybody else.

In his Second Lecture on Discoveries and Inventions, delivered at Jacksonville, Illinois, on February 11, 1859, Mr. Lincoln recognized that self-interest and material gain can prompt an inventor to new discoveries and inventions of high value to mankind. He remarked:

The patent system secured to the inventor, for a limited time, the exclusive use of his invention; and thereby added the fuel of interest to the fire of genius, in the discovery and production of new and useful things.

Competition: Mr. Lincoln firmly believed that every person possesses a fundamental right to work and compete in his or her work with other people for the material goods and comforts of life. In his New Haven speech he declared:

When one starts poor, as most do in the race of life, free society is such that he knows he can better his condition; he knows that there is no fixed condition for labor, for his whole life. I am not ashamed to confess that twenty-five years ago I was a hired laborer, mauling rails, at work on a flatboat—just what might happen to any poor man's son! I want every man to have the chance—and I believe a black man is entitled to it—in which he can better his condition—when he may look forward and hope to be a hired laborer this year and next, work for himself afterward, and finally to hire men to work for him. That is the true system.

Early in his career as a lawyer, Abraham Lincoln delivered an address before the Young Men's Lyceum of Springfield, Illinois. In that speech, The Perpetuation of Our Political Institutions, he spoke as follows about competition among young men of intelligence and ambition:

It is to deny, what the history of the world tells us is true, to suppose that men of ambition and talents will not continue to spring up amongst us. And, when they do, they will as naturally seek the gratification of their ruling passion, as others have so done before them.

The question then, is, can that gratification be found in supporting and maintaining an edifice that has been erected by others? Most certainly it cannot. Many great and good men sufficiently qualified for any task they should undertake, may ever be found, whose ambition would aspire to nothing beyond a seat in Congress, a gubernatorial or a presidential chair; but such belong not to the family of the lion, or the tribe of the eagle.

The above quotation represents Lincoln's early ornate, oratorical style, long before he developed the plain and practical rhetoric of his great presidential speeches. But the same speech contained the following epigram which is often quoted to support his theme that competition among men promotes progress.

Towering genius disdains a beaten path. It seeks regions hitherto unexplored.

Laissez-faire: To what extent should government interfere in the natural economic processes among men to help or thwart any of the three sources (land, labor, capital) of economic production? Lincoln's answer to the question was simple. On July 1, 1854, he wrote:

In all that the people can individually do as well for themselves, the government ought not to interfere.

Competition between labor and capital during the middle of the nineteenth century did not compare, in its intensity, with the competition between those same two segments of the national economy one hundred years later. But the industrial revolution in America was beginning to pose problems during Lincoln's time. Regarding those problems Mr. Lincoln assumed a position that governmental interference would create greater problems and evils than it would solve.

During the 1850s, the industrial revolution in America posed a problem between the use of slave labor in the South and the use of free labor in the North. To compete with slave labor in Southern factories, Northern factory owners reduced wages for free labor. Whereupon free labor in the North began to strike against their employers. The question arose whether or not labor had the right to strike. Should the government deny labor the right to strike?

On March 6, 1860, in his speech at New Haven, Mr. Lincoln tackled the right-to-strike problem as it affected the shoe industry in New England. He said:

I am glad to see that a system of labor prevails in New England under which laborers can strike when they want to, where they are not obliged to work under all circumstances. . . .

Mr. Lincoln was philosophically opposed to having government in any way control labor. In that same regard, he also opposed having the government approve any institution, such as slavery, that would control labor. In the case of slavery, one man as a slave owner would control the labor of another man as a slave. Lincoln believed that free labor meant no ownership of the labor of any man by another man. Also, he supported what is often called the labor theory of value, wherein labor is given credit for creating capital and thereby has greater value. And yet he acknowledged the necessity and importance of capital, as stated in his annual Message to Congress on December 3, 1861.

Labor is prior to, and independent of, capital. Capital is only the fruit of labor, and could never have existed if labor had not first existed. Labor is the superior of capital, and deserves much the higher consideration. Capital has its rights, which are as worthy of protection as any other rights.

Nor is it denied that there is, and probably always will be, a relation between labor and capital, producing mutual benefits. . . . A few men own capital, and that few avoid labor themselves, and, with their capital, hire or buy another few to labor for them. A large majority belong to neither class—neither work for others, nor have others working for them.

Toward the end of that presidential address to Congress, Lincoln summarized his thoughts on freedom of labor and freedom of capital as follows:

The prudent, penniless beginner in the world, labors for wages awhile, saves a surplus with which to buy tools or land for himself; then labors on his own account another while, and at length hires another new beginner to help him. This is the just, and generous, and prosperous system which opens the way to all—gives hope to all, and consequent energy, and progress, and improvement of condition to all.

No men living are more worthy to be trusted than those who toil up from poverty—none less inclined to take, or touch, aught which they have not honestly earned.

Let them beware of surrendering a political power which they already possess, and which, if surrendered, will surely be used to close the door of advancement against such as they, and to fix new disabilities and burdens upon them, till all of liberty shall be lost.

One of the popular photographs of Lincoln, showing the President wearing spectacles. Standing with Lincoln is his son, Tad. This photograph was taken by Anthony Berger in Mathew Brady's Gallery in Washington, D.C., on February 9, 1864. *Courtesy of the Illinois State Historical Library, Old State Capitol, Springfield, Illinois.*

44

Quotations on Freedom

As history has identified the final character of all men everywhere, the character of Abraham Lincoln has become revealed as a devotion by a humble man to three great ideals which were: a belief in freedom; a belief in God; a belief in forgiveness.

Of the three great philosophical convictions for which Abraham Lincoln stood, the one which the world remembers best is his belief in the personal freedom of the individual. At a time in United States history when the institution of slavery was being extended into the new territories of Kansas and Nebraska, Mr. Lincoln took the stand that slavery was morally wrong and should not be extended.

Prior to the famous Lincoln-Douglas debates of 1858, the events which surrounded the issue of slavery or freedom for the black man in America included:

1. The Ordinance of 1787 which prohibited slavery in the Northwest Territory.
2. The Louisiana Purchase of 1803.
3. The Missouri Compromise of 1820 which admitted Missouri to the Union as a slave state, and which stated that all new territories and states created out of the Louisiana Purchase north of 36° 30′ should be free from slavery.
4. The Mexican Cession of 1848 following the U.S. War with Mexico.
5. The Compromise of 1850 which provided:
   a. California was admitted as a free state. (This provision favored the North)

b. Popular sovereignty for New Mexico and Utah territories when admitted as states. (This provision favored the South)

c. Prohibition of the slave trade in District of Columbia. (This provision favored the North)

d. A Fugitive Slave Law compelling northern states to return runaway slaves to legal owners. (This provision favored the South)

e. The size of Texas was reduced. (This provision favored the North)

f. Texas war debt (for war against Mexico) was paid up to $10,000,000 by the U.S. Government. (This provision favored the South)

6. Nebraska petitioned in 1853 for territorial status:

a. The original bill made no mention of slavery.

b. Senator Douglas's second bill provided for popular sovereignty, and stipulated the specific repeal of the Missouri Compromise.

7. Douglas promoted popular sovereignty because:

a. The South would support any hope for extending slavery.

b. The North would support any reason for extending a railroad into new territories westward from Chicago (instead of westward from New Orleans).

c. Douglas had aspirations for the presidency.

d. Douglas expected that climate, soil, and industry would preclude slavery from being established in Kansas and Nebraska.

8. The Kansas-Nebraska Bill, including popular sovereignty, passed Congress after four months of debate. Supporting arguments for its passage were:

a. A new basis was needed for organizing territories.

b. Popular sovereignty was a principle already established by the Compromise of 1850 for Utah and New Mexico territories.

c. Popular sovereignty was intrinsically right under the U.S. Constitution.

9. Abraham Lincoln opposed the Kansas-Nebraska bill with its doctrine of popular sovereignty. His stand was:

a. Slavery in our first national domain, the Northwest Territory, was prohibited by the Ordinance of 1787.

b. The Missouri Compromise of 1820 and the Compromise of 1850 preserved much newly acquired territory as free territory into which slavery could not be extended.

c. Extending slavery into Kansas and Nebraska territories denied the civil liberties of those citizens who believed that slavery was morally wrong.

10. Defense of his stand against extending slavery was made by Lincoln, prior to the Great Debates, at:

a. Springfield, October 4, 1854, during the Illinois State Fair, in answer to Senator Douglas's position on popular sovereignty and the Kansas Nebraska Act.

b. Peoria, October 16, 1854, in answer to Senator Douglas's defense of popular sovereignty and the Kansas-Nebraska Act.

c. Bloomington, May 29, 1856 (the Lost Speech).
d. Springfield, June 26, 1857, in answer to Senator Douglas's defense of the Dred Scott decision.
e. Springfield, June 16, 1858. This was Lincoln's House Divided Speech made in his acceptance of the Republican nomination for U.S. Senator, running against incumbent Senator Douglas.
f. Chicago, July 10, 1858, answering Senator Douglas, and beginning the campaign for the U.S. Senate.

The Lincoln-Douglas debates, during the late summer and early fall of 1858, were the first public discussions in depth of the issue of the extension of slavery in the United States. Locations and dates for the debates were:

1. Ottawa, August 21, 1858   *Douglas spoke first.*
2. Freeport, August 27, 1858 *Lincoln spoke first.*
3. Jonesboro, September 15, 1858 *Douglas spoke first.*
4. Charleston, September 18, 1858 *Lincoln spoke first.*
5. Galesburg, October 7, 1858 *Douglas spoke first.*
6. Quincy, October 13, 1858 *Lincoln spoke first.*
7. Alton, October 15, 1858 *Douglas spoke first.*

In the chapter on Quotations on Logical Thinking under the heading of Premises in Lincoln's Thinking, several quotations from Lincoln may be repeated here as supporting Lincoln's belief in freedom. Additional quotations from Lincoln confirming his fundamental belief in freedom should include:

If the Negro is a man, then my ancient faith teaches me that "all men are created equal," and that there can be no moral right in connection with one man's making a slave of another.

The above quotation from Lincoln was made at Peoria, Illinois, on October 16, 1854. On the previous day, Senator Stephen A. Douglas had defended his sponsorship of the Kansas-Nebraska Act which specifically repealed the Missouri Compromise of 1820 and organized both Kansas and Nebraska territories for settlement under popular sovereignty. Lincoln stressed the moral wrongness of slavery and vigorously opposed its extension into the territories.

One of Lincoln's most frequently quoted statements on freedom was written during the summer of 1858 when he penciled some Notes on Slavery in preparation for the Lincoln-Douglas Debates. Dated August 1, 1858, the famous comment was:

As I would not be a slave, so I would not be a master. This expresses my ideal of democracy. Whatever differs from this, to the extent of the difference, is no democracy.

The following opinion was made by Lincoln during the fifth debate which was held at Knox College in Galesburg, Illinois, October 7, 1858:

I believe that the right of property in a slave is not distinctly and expressly affirmed in the Constitution.

During the sixth debate at Quincy, Illinois, October 13, 1858, Lincoln focused on the moral aspects of slavery, saying:

The difference of opinion, reduced to its terms, is no other than the difference between the men who think slavery a wrong, and those who do not think it a wrong.

The seventh and last of the Lincoln-Douglas debates was held at Alton, Illinois, October 15, 1858, where Lincoln summarized his stand on the morality of slavery.

It is the eternal struggle between these two principles—right and wrong—throughout the world. No matter in what shape it comes, whether from the mouth of a king who seeks to bestride the people of his own nation and live by the fruit of their labor, or from one race of men as an apology for enslaving another race, it is the same tyrannical principle.

In a letter which Lincoln wrote to Henry L. Pierce on April 6, 1859, the following quotation is worthy of special notice:

This is a world of compensation; and he who would be no slave must consent to have no slave. Those who deny freedom to others deserve it not for themselves, and under a just God, cannot long retain it.

The most memorable statement in the Emancipation Proclamation of January 1, 1863, is the following:

That on the first day of January, in the year of our Lord one thousand eight hundred and sixty-three, all persons held as slaves within any State, or designated part of a State, the people whereof shall then be in rebellion against the United States, shall be then, thenceforward, and forever free.

As Lincoln related his belief in freedom to his concepts of democracy, the following quotation from his Gettysburg Address of November 19, 1863 will always be remembered:

That we here highly resolve that these dead shall not have died in vain; that this nation, under God, shall have a new birth of freedom; that government of the people, by the people, for the people, shall not perish from the earth.

On March 17, 1865, when the Civil War was within a month from ending at Appomattox Court House in Virginia, the 140th Indiana Regiment stopped at the White House to serenade the president. Included in Lincoln's remarks to the regiment was the following comment:

I have always thought that all men should be free; but if any should be slaves, it should be first those who desire it for themselves, and secondly, those who desire it for others. Whenever I hear anyone arguing for slavery, I feel a strong impulse to see it tried on him personally.

Four days before his assassination, this last photograph of President Abraham Lincoln was taken in Washington, D.C. by Alexander Gardner on April 10, 1865. On the previous day, General Lee had surrendered his Confederate army to the Union General U. S. Grant. Scholars often contemplate the faint peaceful smile on Lincoln's face and the far-away look in his eye. *Courtesy of the Illinois State Historical Library, Old State Capitol, Springfield, Illinois.*

50

Quotations on God

When Abraham Lincoln was campaigning in 1846 as the Whig candidate for Congress, some of his critics accused him of not being a religious man. The fact that Lincoln was not an active member of any church was a factor in favor of his opponent, the Rev. Peter Cartwright. Lincoln finally felt compelled to answer the criticism. He did so by releasing the following handbill:

To the Voters of the Seventh Congressional District

Fellow Citizens: A charge having got into circulation in some of the neighborhoods of this District, in substance that I am an open scoffer of Christianity, I have by the advice of some friends concluded to notice the subject in this form. That I am not a member of any Christian Church, is true; but I have never denied the truth of the Scriptures; and I have never spoken with intentional disrespect of religion in general, or of any denomination of Christians in particular.

It is true that in early life I was inclined to believe in what I understand is called the Doctrine of Necessity, that is, the human mind is impelled to action, or held in rest, by some power, over which the mind itself has no control; and I have sometimes (with one, two, or three, but never publicly) tried to maintain this opinion in argument. The habit of arguing thus, however, I have entirely left off for more than five years. And I add here, I have always understood this same opinion to be held by several of the Christian denominations. The foregoing is the whole truth, briefly stated, ...

I do not think I could myself be brought to

support a man for office whom I knew to be an open enemy of, and scoffer at, religion.

In his speeches, letters, and official public proclamations, Abraham Lincoln made hundreds of references to God or to a Supreme Being.

In *Reminiscences of Lincoln*, by Joshua Speed, who was one of Lincoln's closest friends, the following statement by Lincoln is quoted:

I am profitably engaged in reading the Bible. Take all of this Book (the Bible) upon reason that you can, and the balance on faith, and you will live and die a happier and better man.

Young Abe Lincoln grew up in a strongly religious atmosphere. In 1816, when Thomas Lincoln and his family moved from Kentucky to southern Indiana, Abe was only seven years old. The family Bible was closely guarded in their home. Two years later Nancy Hanks Lincoln died of the "milk-sick," (typhoid fever) and Abe and his sister Sarah remained without motherly care until Thomas Lincoln returned to Elizabethtown, Kentucky, and married Sarah Bush Johnston, a widow with three children. Together Thomas and Sarah Bush Lincoln helped to establish the Pigeon Creek Baptist Church near Gentryville, Indiana. Religious teachings from the Bible comprised a goodly part of the encouragement which young Abraham received from his stepmother. Sermons at the church were mostly of the hellfire-and-brimstone variety and clung to the separate Baptist faith that all people and events had been predestined by a Supreme God. According to a report by Abe's stepsister, Matilda Johnston, after Abe had attended church with his parents, he would search out a stump from which he would repeat, for the neighborhood children, the sermon word for word and gesture for gesture.

By the time that the Thomas Lincolns moved to Illinois in 1830, Abraham Lincoln had become of age. After helping his father to clear some land and build a cabin about five miles west of Decatur, he left home. But the strong religious influence of his father, mother, stepmother remained with him for life. Basically he was a predestinarian Baptist. As he once commented in later years to Congressman Isaac Newton Arnold, "I have been all my life a fatalist."

On February 1, 1850, Edward Baker Lincoln, age four, the second son of Abraham and Mary Todd Lincoln, died of consumption. Prior to that time Mr. Lincoln and his wife had occasionally attended the Episcopal Church in Springfield. But at the time of Eddie's death, the Episcopal minister, Rev. Charles Dresser, was out of town. The Lincolns then asked the Rev. James Smith, Minister of the First Presbyterian Church to conduct the funeral services for their son. That somber occasion began a strong relationship between Mr. Lincoln and Rev. Smith. Some writers have reported that after Edward died Mr. Lincoln and his wife regularly attended the Presbyterian Church. Other writers have stated that because Mr. Lincoln was away from home so much by riding the Eighth Judicial Circuit, he seldom attended church with Mrs. Lincoln. At any rate, starting shortly after Edward's funeral, Mr. Lincoln did rent a pew in the Church for $50 a year.

The Rev. James Smith had written a book entitled, *The Christian Defense*. Lincoln's legal mind was so impressed with its contents that, according to William J. Wolf, he announced to some friends:

I have been reading a work of Dr. Smith on the evidence of Christianity, and have heard him preach and converse on the subject, and I am now convinced of the truth of the Christian religion.

Occasionally Lincoln attended special revival meetings at Rev. Smith's Church, and in 1852, Lincoln even gave a lecture on the Bible to a men's meeting in the church. Although Mrs. Lincoln reportedly joined the church, Mr. Lincoln did not.

By the time that Abraham Lincoln reentered politics after the passage of the Kansas-Nebraska Act in 1854, his fundamental belief in freedom had become anchored to the Declaration of Independence concept "that all men are created equal; that they are endowed by their Creator with certain inalienable rights." Throughout the Lincoln-Douglas Debates of 1858, Lincoln repeatedly emphasized that "all men were created equal," and that the "inalienable rights" of all men, including blacks, were "endowed by their Creator."

On July 10, 1858, during his speech at Chicago, Illinois, Abraham Lincoln made the following statement pertaining to a Divine Providence:

It is said in one of the admonitions of the Lord, "As your Father in Heaven is perfect, be ye also perfect." The Savior, I suppose, did not expect that any human creature could be perfect as the Father in Heaven. He set that up as a standard, and he who did most toward reaching that standard attained the highest degree of moral perfection.

In his Farewell Address at Springfield, Illinois, on February 11, 1861, the president-elect made special reference to the Divine Being to whom he asked his friends to offer their prayers:

I now leave, with a task before me greater than that which rested upon Washington. Without the assistance of that Divine Being, who ever attended him, I cannot succeed. With that assistance I cannot fail.

On March 4, 1861, President Lincoln's First Inaugural Address was a plea for any dissatisfied countrymen who were contemplating civil war to "think calmly and well upon this subject. Nothing valuable can be lost by taking time." Concerning the relationship of Almighty God to the righteousness of the cause of each opposing side in the threatened conflict, the president said:

In our present differences, is either party without faith of being in the right? If the Almighty Ruler of nations, with His eternal truth and justice, be on your side of the North, or on yours of the South, that truth, and that justice, will surely prevail by the judgment of this great tribunal, the American people.

Appealing to all dissatisfied countrymen, Lincoln argued:

If it were admitted that you who are dissatisfied hold the right side of the dispute, there still is no single good reason for precipitate action.

Identifying four bases, including a belief in God, for settling the pending intersectional strife, the president implored:

Intelligence, patriotism, Christianity, and a firm reliance on Him, who has never yet forsaken this favored land, are still competent to adjust, in the best way, all our present difficulty.

During his second year in the White House, the horrors of the Civil War deepened Lincoln's confidence that God's will would settle the issue of slavery throughout the nation. And when his young son, William Wallace Lincoln, age twelve, died at the White House from typhoid fever on February 20, 1862, Lincoln's grief found comfort only from the belief that the death had been God's will, and that his own responsibility as president could be performed better only by trying harder to know God's will.

In Washington, D.C., the Lincolns rented a pew in the New York Avenue Presbyterian Church. The Minister there was Dr. Phineas D. Gurley who conducted the services for Willie's funeral, and eventually conducted the Washington D.C. memorial services for the martyred president.

Gloom swept the North following the Union Army defeat at the Second Battle of Bull Run on August 29, 1862. But Lincoln expressed a firm belief that Confederate General Lee and his invading army in Pennsylvania could and would be defeated. On September 16-17, 1862, the Battle of Antietam turned into a Union victory after Lee began to retreat toward Virginia. One week later, on September 22, President Lincoln made his preliminary announcement for the Emancipation Proclamation. The Union victory at Antietam provided stability and future success for the federal government. At the close of his announcement, Lincoln said:

I made a solemn vow before God that if General Lee was driven back from Pennsylvania, I would crown the result by the declaration of freedom to the slaves.

Lincoln looked upon his proclamation as his responsibility to God and man, and as gratitude to God for the first sign of success in achieving the goal of freedom for all men.

In order to promote "a due regard for the Divine," on November 15, 1862, President Lincoln proclaimed an Order for Sabbath Observance, stating:

The President. . . . desires and enjoins the orderly observance of the Sabbath by the officers and men in the military and naval service. . . .the sacred rights of Christian soldiers and sailors, a becoming deference to the best sentiment of a Christian people, and a due regard for the Divine, will demand that Sunday labor in the army and navy be reduced to the measure of strict necessity.

In his *Recollections of President Lincoln*, L. E. Chittenden recalled Abraham Lincoln making the following general appraisal of the Holy Bible:

Now let us treat the Bible fairly. If we had a witness on the stand whose general story we knew was true, we would believe him when he asserted facts of which we had no other evidence. We ought to treat the Bible with equal fairness. I decided a long time ago that it was less difficult to believe that the Bible was what it claimed to be than to disbelieve it. It is a good book for us to obey. It contains the Ten Commandments, the Golden Rule, and other rules which ought to be followed. No man was ever the worse for living according to the directions of the Bible.

As reported by Francis B. Carpenter in his book *Six Months at the White House with Abraham Lincoln*, the president once rebuked a minister who expressed the hope that the Lord was on the side of the North in the Civil War. Lincoln's response was:

I don't agree with you. I am not at all concerned about that, for I know that the Lord is always on the side of the right. But it is my constant anxiety and prayer that I and this nation should be on the Lord's side.

Lincoln's lack of direct membership in any organized denomination of Christianity was due to his reticence to accept particular rituals and dogmas in popular church services. As reported by Edgar DeWitt Jones in *Lincoln and the Preachers*, the president once responded to Congressman Henry C. Deming, saying:

I have never united myself to any church, because I have found difficulty in giving my assent, without mental reservation, to the long complicated statements of Christian doctrine which characterize their article of belief and confessions of faith.

When any church will inscribe over its altars, as its sole qualification for membership, the Savior's condensed statement of the substance of both law and gospel, "Thou shalt love the Lord thy God with all thy heart, and with all thy soul, and with all thy mind, and thy neighbor as thyself," that church will I join with all my heart and all my soul.

In Lincoln's letter to Thurlow Weed, March 15, 1865, the following comment is found:

Men are not flattered by being shown that there has been a difference of purpose between the Almighty and them. To deny it, however, in this case, is to deny that there is a God governing the world. It is a truth which I thought needed to be told, and, as whatever of humiliation there is in it [that] fall most directly on myself, I thought others might afford for me to tell it.

Two days after General Lee surrendered the remaining 25,000 men and officers of his Confederate Army to the Union Army of General Grant, President Lincoln at the White House addressed a large crowd that came to serenade him. In what became known as Lincoln's Last Public Address (only three days before his assassination), the president was fully mindful of man's need to be humble before God, saying:

In the midst of this, however, He from whom all blessings flow, must not be forgotten. A call for a national thanksgiving is being prepared, and will be duly promulgated.

President Lincoln's Second Inaugural Address at Washington, D.C., March 4, 1865, has been appraised as "the only known perfect example of the spoken English language." Approximately one half of the three-minute speech dealt with references to God, the Bible, the Almighty, and the Lord. That part of the address, expressing Lincoln's belief in God, follows:

. . . . Both [sides in the conflict] read the same Bible, and pray to the same God; and each invokes His aid against the other. It may seem strange that any men should dare to ask a just God's assistance in wringing their bread from the sweat of other men's faces; but let us judge not, that we be not judged. The prayers of

neither have been answered fully. The Almighty has His own purposes.

Woe unto the world because of offenses, for it must needs be that offenses come; but woe to that man by whom the offense cometh. If we shall suppose that American slavery is one of those offenses which, in the providence of God, must needs come, but which, having continued through His appointed time, He now wills to remove, and that He gives to both North and South this terrible war, as the woe due to those by whom the offense came, shall we discern therein any departure from those divine attributes which the believers in the living God always ascribe to Him?

Fondly do we hope—fervently do we pray—that this mighty scourge of war may speedily pass away. Yet, if God wills that it continue until all the wealth piled by the bondsman's 250 years of unrequited toil shall be sunk, and until every drop of blood drawn with the lash shall be paid by another drawn with the sword, as was said 3,000 years ago, so still it must be said: "The judgments of the Lord are true and righteous altogether."

With malice toward none; with Charity for all; with firmness in the right, as God gives us to see the right, let us strive on. . . .

Statue by Daniel C. French, made in 1922.
Lincoln Memorial, Washington, D.C. *Courtesy of
the Illinois State Historical Library, Old State
Capitol, Springfield, Illinois.*

58

Quotations on Forgiveness

How should a person act toward an adversary who has lost a contest? In victory, should the winner further punish the defeated contender and make him pay for the cost and the pain of the contest? Or should the winner forgive the loser for the damage that he has done? And if forgiveness is the answer, should the winner then help the loser to rehabilitate himself?

Those were the broad and timeless philosophical questions which bothered President Lincoln all during the Civil War. But as soon as he was certain that eventually the Union would triumph over the rebellious Confederate states, he did not hesitate to announce his policies of reconstruction for the South.

On July 4, 1863, Union armies under General George Meade defeated the Confederate forces of General Robert E. Lee at Gettysburg, Pennsylvania. On the same day, General U. S. Grant's armies in the West captured the fortress town of Vicksburg on the Mississippi River. Those two important Union victories pointed toward an eventual defeat for the southern Confederacy.

With Union victory appearing certain, leaders in the Senate and House of Representatives began to demand that, when the war ended, the South should be punished for making war upon the Union. So many families had lost sons or fathers in the war that most Congressmen were pressured by their constituents to make the rebels pay for the death and destruction they brought upon the nation.

In the Senate, the leader of the majority party was Republican Charles Sumner of Massachussetts. As a brilliant statesman who took his duties seriously,

Sumner listened carefully to the anguished pleadings of constituents who demanded retribution for the losses they suffered. In order to allow Congress to set up "conditions" (punishments) for bringing the defeated rebel states back into the Union, Sumner conceived the State Suicide Theory which he propounded in the nine resolutions which he introduced into the Senate.

The first of Sumner's nine resolutions, in support of his State Suicide Theory, read as follows:

1. Resolved: that any vote of secession or other act, by which any state may put an end to the supremacy of the Constitution within its territory, is inoperative and void against the Constitution, and when sustained by force it becomes a practical abdication by the State of all rights under the Constitution, while the treason which it involves still further works an instant forfeiture of all those functions and powers essential to the continued existence of the State as a body politic,. . . .

No spirit of compassion or conciliation could be detected in the language of the nine resolutions proposed by Sumner. Only the spirit of retribution and punishment prevailed. Although the nine resolutions were not passed as an act of Congress, they did form the basis for the Congressional Plan (the Wade-Davis Bill) which was passed by Congress on July 4, 1864.

Congressman Thaddeus Stevens of Pennsylvania, in the House of Representatives, formulated his Conquered Territories Doctrine for punishing the South. Stevens began his chain of reasoning with two assumptions: 1. A territory by coming into the Union became a state; 2. A state by going out of the Union became a territory. Thus, Stevens looked upon each of the seceded states as federal territories. Futhermore, since they took up arms against the Union, they were subject to being conquered as any common enemy could be conquered.

The severity of the Conquered Territories doctrine can be understood by observing various proposed applications of it. As Chairman of the House Committee on Ways and Means, Stevens proposed an appropriation bill for paying officers to collect revenues in States which did not belong to the Union. He defended his bill before Congress by saying:

I propose to levy that tax and collect it as a war measure. I would levy a tax wherever I can upon these conquered provinces, just as all nations levy them upon provinces and nations they conquer. If my views and principles are right, I would not only collect that tax, but I would, as a necessary war measure, take every particle of property, real and personal, life estate and reversion, of every disloyal man, and sell it for the benefit of the nation in carrying on this war. We have such power, and we are to treat them simply as provinces to be conquered, and as a nation fighting in hostility to us until we do conquer them.

The response of President Lincoln to demands for punishment against the South was a strong stand in favor of amnesty toward the South. In Lincoln's mind, Reconstruction must include the pardoning of most of the citizens in the rebellious states in order to restore those states to full statehood in the Union.

In his annual message to Congress, December 8, 1863, Lincoln surprised his listeners by announcing that he was issuing, on the same day, a proclamation providing for amnesty and local elections in those portions of the South where Confederate control had been defeated or withdrawn (see Appendix, Part 3, Message No. 8, Proclamation of Amnesty and Reconstruction).

Lincoln's philosophical approach to the problem was that of forgiveness, while Congress was trying to create plans for punishment. Also, Lincoln assumed that constitutionally the seceded states had never really left the Union, and that Congress possessed no constitutional authority for changing basic provisions for their membership in the Union.

In summary, Lincoln's Proclamation of Amnesty and Reconstruction had three main provisions:

1. Amnesty was promised to all persons who participated in the rebellion, excepting certain described classes, upon taking an oath which pledged support of:
   a. The Constitution and the Union
   b. Congressioal legislation on slavery during the war.
   c. Executive proclamations on slavery.
2. Reinstatement of statehood was promised to a rebellious state whenever a number of its citizens . . . should reestablish a state government in conformity with provisions of the prescribed oath of allegiance.
3. Permanent freedom was assured to the emancipated race of slaves in all states that had been in rebellion. Although Lincoln's proclamation did not grant the elective franchise to the freedmen (nor could it do so under the Constitution, since the several states determined the elective franchise within their borders), nevertheless he favored granting the franchise to those freedmen who fought in the Union armies and to other freedmen who met the general requirements for electors in the several states.

The reasons for President Lincoln's belief in amnesty and reconstruction can be summarized as follows.

1. A state could not legally, according to its own constitution, leave the Union. As Lincoln stated in his First Inaugural Address:

   . . . . no government proper ever had a provision in its organic law for its own termination.

2. Resolutions by a state legislature could not remove a state from the Union. As stated in the First Inaugural Address:

   No state, upon its mere motion, can, lawfully get out of the Union: resolves and ordinances to that effect are legally void.

3. The majority of the Southern people opposed disunion but were forced into secession by radical leaders who took over control of their state government.
4. Disloyal leaders in most of the Southern states represented a minority of the people in each state.
5. Peaceful, loyal citizens in any seceded state should be given protection by the federal government.
6. Southern leaders who fostered sedition could be tried in court, and, if guilty, punished.
7. Simple restoration of statehood and citizenship to

all loyal people of the seceded states would avoid a multiplicity of problems under other plans.

8. As soon as federal power overcame armed resistance in any state, reconstruction could begin. Military governors caused many problems that could have been avoided by reinstated statehood and amnesty.

9. Lincoln's plan was already working in West Virginia.

10. A spirit of compassion and forgiveness toward the South by the North would help to heal the wounds of war more quickly than punishment. Amnesty was honest and manly. It was Christian. It was the Golden Rule applied to statesmanship.

Numerous plans were introduced before Congress for Reconstruction of the South, but not one of them was passed until July 1864 when the so-called Congressional Plan (the Wade-Davis Bill) was adopted. Both the State Suicide theory of Sumner and the Conquered Territories doctrine of Stevens exerted their influence in formulating the Congressional Plan which provided for a complicated system of Congressional approvals, including certain right conditions, for admitting a rebellious state back into the Union.

Passage of the Wade-Davis Bill was a slap in the face to President Lincoln because it encompassed provisions which would enable the vindictive North to punish a vanquished South. Also, it included attempts by Congress to claim for itself certain administrative functions of the president, and to decide by itself certain constitutional matters which should be settled by ratification of constitutional amendments by the several states.

President Lincoln refused to sign the Wade-Davis Act. When it was presented to him on July 4, 1864, in the president's room of the National Capitol Building, he laid it aside and went on with the signing of other bills. Senators Sumner, Boutwell, and Chandler had come to witness the signature, and, if necessary, to urge the signing. When Mr. Lincoln's determination not to sign the bill became evident, the senators implored him to do so for the sake of prohibiting slavery in the reconstructed states. To which pleading the president replied:

> That is the point on which I doubt the authority of Congress to act. I conceive that I may in an emergency do things on military grounds which cannot be done Constitutionally by Congress.

Chagrined, the senators departed, but before they left Washington to return to their respective states, several of them conspired to issue a public condemnation of the president.

In speaking to his cabinet members who also attended the meeting, the president commented further:

> This bill and the position of these gentlemen seem to me, in asserting that the insurrectionary States are no longer in the Union, to make the fatal admission that States, whenever they please, may of their own motion dissolve their connection with the Union. Now we cannot survive that admission, I am convinced. It was to obviate this question that I earnestly favored the movement for an amendment to the

Constitution abolishing slavery, which passed the Senate and failed in the House. I thought it much better, if it were possible, to restore the Union without the necessity of a violent quarrel among its friends as to whether certain States have been in or out of the Union during the war—a mere metaphysical question, and one unnecessary to be forced into discussion.

Even though his veto of the Wade-Davis Bill was certain to dismay many of the national leaders, nevertheless he vetoed the bill because of five reasons:

1. The bill wrongly assumed that Congress possessed constitutional authority to abolish slavery. Lincoln favored a constitutional amendment on the issue.

2. The bill assumed that states, on their own initiative, could withdraw from the Union. Lincoln denied that the states could legally secede from the Union.

3. The bill stipulated a procedure for statehood reinstatement which could allow Congress to add conditions which might easily reflect Congressional vindictiveness against the South.

4. The bill would replace the basis on which Arkansas and Louisiana had already rejoined the Union.

5. The bill would encourage further confederate military resistance to federal authority instead of encouraging an earlier rejoining of the Union under amnesty.

Between the time that Congress adjourned on July 4, 1864 and the time that it reconvened on December 5, the chief authors of the Congressional Plan publicly displayed their contempt for President Lincoln's refusal to sign their plan into law. On August 5, Senator Wade and Congressman Davis issued a joint protest which was printed in the *New York Tribune*. Their bitter attack against the president was addressed To the Supporters of the Government. Excerpts include:

A more studied outrage on the legislative authority of the people has never been perpetrated. Congress passed a bill: the President refused to sign it, and then by proclamation puts as much of it in force as he sees fit.

The President has greatly presumed on the forbearance which the supporters of his administration have so long practiced. But he must understand that our support is of a cause, and not of a man; that the authority of Congress is paramount and must be respected; that the whole body of the Union men of Congress will not submit to be impeached by him of rash and unconstitutional legislation; and if he wishes our support, he must confine himself to his Executive duties;—to obey and execute, not make the laws—to suppress by arms armed rebellion, and leave political reorganization to Congress.

If the supporters of the Government fail to insist on this, they become responsible for the usurpations which they fail to rebuke, and are justly liable to the indignation of the people whose rights and security, committed to their keeping, they sacrifice. Let them consider the remedy for these usurpations, and having found it, fearlessly execute it.

What did the renowned senator and congressman mean by the words "the remedy for these usurpations," and the words "fearlessly execute it"? Did they mean for fellow Republicans not to vote for Lincoln in the autumn election? If that was what they meant, they could have said so explicitly. At least a more menacing interpretation was not ruled out.

When Congress reassembled on December 5, 1864, Mr. Lincoln had been elected president for a second term. The war was, at last, grinding down to a halt. In the West, the Confederacy was defeated. Arkansas and Louisiana had been recognized by the president to have rejoined the Union. Military governors were administering federal authority in Tennessee and Mississippi. The Confederate battleship *Alabama* had been sunk and the battleship *Florida* had been captured, thus ending further annoyance to Union shipping. General Sherman was leading his Union army through Georgia, crushing the last vestiges of Confederate military opposition in the South. In Virginia, General Grant was driving the Confederate forces under General Lee back into the defenses around Richmond and Petersburg.

The final and complete military defeat of the Confederacy was expected within only a few months after Congress reassembled. But the mood of Congress was not friendly toward the president. In fact, hostility toward Mr. Lincoln had intensified. The more radical leaders in Congress were still determined to force the president to accept their own Congressional plans for reconstruction.

President Lincoln's unequivocal defense of his policy of Reconstruction With Amnesty was made in his Second Inaugural Address, March 4, 1865. Only the mind and the soul of Abraham Lincoln could phrase that policy in those poetical and immortal words:

With malice toward none; with Charity for all;

As his second term in the presidency began, his announced policy of amnesty toward the vanquished South became an obsession with Abraham Lincoln. Three weeks following his second inauguration, the president left the capital, sailed down the Potomac River on the *River Queen*, and arrived on March 24, at City Point, Virginia, General Grant's Union Army Headquarters near the mouth of the James River. Three days later, the president met with General Grant, General Sherman, and Admiral Porter in the cabin of the admiral's flagship for a conference which lasted late into the night and continued on the following day.

At this final top-level military meeting on March 27 and 28, 1865, the surrender terms for the Confederate armies, and general plans of reconstruction with amnesty, were outlined by the president. Then the generals returned to their troops, and the president sent telegrams to Secretary of War Stanton directing the arrangements for the raising of the flag over Fort Sumter on April 14, exactly four years after Major Robert Anderson had surrendered the fort to General Beauregard.

On April 1, 1865, General Lee made his final attack against Union forces. The Battle of Five Forks, near Petersburg, was a decided victory for General Sheridan who had joined forces with General Grant. The president remained at City Point, and on April 2, he visited the battlefront near Petersburg. He was determined to observe the first applications of his policy of amnesty toward a conquered and surrendering people.

On April 3, the city of Richmond, capital of the Confederacy, fell to Union forces. The very next day, with the city still in flames, President Lincoln, protected by a guard of only ten Marines, entered the city on foot. For two days he stayed at the former house of Confederate President Jefferson Davis while Union occupation forces began the ugly job of policing a conquered people. To General Godfrey Weitzel, the commanding Union officer of Richmond, the president offered the suggestion:

If I were in your place, General, I'd let 'em up easy; let 'em up easy.

On Saturday, April 8, Lincoln began his return trip to Washington, D.C. On Sunday April 9, he visited Secretary of State Seward who had been injured in a carriage accident. On the same day, at Appomattox Court House, Virginia, General Lee surrendered to General Grant.

Reports reached Washington that General Grant's terms of surrender were unbelievably lenient. Instead of taking as prisoners the surrendering 25,000 troops, all of General Lee's men were allowed to return to their homes, taking their horses and mules for spring plowing, and officers were permitted to retain their sidearms! And to the hungry soldiers of the disbanding Confederate Army, General Grant distributed 25,000 rations of food. President Lincoln's policy of reconstruction with amnesty had begun.

President Lincoln's Last Public Address was delivered from the front of the White House where an immense crowd gathered the evening of April ll. The speech dealt mainly with amnesty, the President declaring:

We meet this evening, not in sorrow, but in gladness of heart. The evacuation of Petersburg and Richmond, and the surrender of the principal insurgent army, give hope of a righteous and speedy peace whose joyous expression cannot be restrained. In the midst of this, however, He, from Whom all blessings flow, must not be forgotten. A call for a national thanksgiving is being prepared, and will be duly promulgated. . . .

We all agree that the seceded States, so called, are out of their proper practical relation with the Union; and that the sole object of the government, civil and military, in regard to those States is to again get them into that proper practical relation. I believe it is not only possible, but in fact, easier, to do this, without deciding, or even considering, whether these states have even been out of the Union, than with it. Finding themselves safely at home, it would be utterly immaterial whether they had ever been abroad. Let us all join in doing the acts necessary to restoring the proper practical relations between these states and the Union; and each forever after, innocently indulge his own opinion whether, in doing the acts, he brought the States from without, into the Union, or only gave them proper assistance, they never having been out of it. . . .

At the end of the president's speech New York Senator Ira Harris in the crowd asked: "What are you going to do with the rebel leaders?" Immediately the crowd set up a chant, "Hang them! Hang them! Hang them!" The president's young son, Tad, aged eleven, tugged on his father's sleeve and cried, "No papa! Don't hang them. Hang onto them." Raising his hands to quiet the crowd, the president declared emphatically:

There! Tad's got it! Don't hang them! Hang onto them!

And the crowd, some of which had hoped to hear vengeance declared, slowly drifted away.

On Wednesday, April 12, public celebrations spread all over the North. But various members of Congress conferred with Lincoln to protest his amnesty toward the South. Senator Sumner was still disturbed. And even Lincoln's Secretary of War, Edwin M. Stanton, protested to the president that the fruits of victory were being given away. As Stanton interpreted Lincoln's amnesty policy at Appomattox, it was not Lee who surrendered to Grant, but Grant who surrendered to Lee.

Thursday, April 13, was only three days before Easter. Public rejoicing continued to grow. In addition to a heavy schedule of meetings, President Lincoln wrote six messages including a Memorandum Respecting Reduction of the Regular Army which he gave to Stanton. On the basis of the memorandum, Stanton issued an order to stop the drafting of citizens for service in the armed forces. Truly, peace was returning to the country.

Good Friday, April 14, 1865, was a beautiful spring day in Washington, D.C. Dogwood trees and lilacs were in blossom. Everywhere the spirit of a new life was felt by the people. The war was over.

Richmond had fallen. Lee had surrendered. Jefferson Davis and his cabinet had fled. To where? Nobody cared. And the military draft had ended. The war was over!

Jubilation was everywhere in the North on that beautiful day. At Fort Sumter in Charleston Harbor, South Carolina, an impressive ceremony, instigated by President Lincoln, raised the same Union flag that had been hauled down exactly four years before. Main speakers on that occasion were Henry Ward Beecher, William Lloyd Garrison, and General Robert Anderson, the Union commander who, as a major, had previously surrendered the fort.

For Abraham Lincoln the day was too heavily scheduled with work for any rejoicing until evening. By seven o'clock in the morning, he was in his office answering his mail. He sent General Grant a note asking him to attend the cabinet meeting scheduled for eleven o'clock. He also wrote twelve other messages later in the day. At breakfast with Mrs. Lincoln and son Tad, he was gladdened by the visit of his oldest son, Robert Todd Lincoln, who had just arrived in the capital, coming from Appomattox where he had been an aide to General Grant. For the first time during his presidency, Abraham Lincoln felt happy. All day he radiated good feeling, good humor, and good confidence in the future.

At the eleven o'clock cabinet meeting, the president introduced General Grant for a report on the windup of the war. The second half of the meeting was spent by Lincoln explaining the many ramifications of his policy of reconstruction. He discusssed such questions as: How could civil government be restored in Southern states? How should the federal government deal with the rebel leaders? How could trade be restored between the North and South?

According to Gideon Welles, the secretary of the navy, who kept a diary of daily happenings during the Civil War, the president emphasized that he would not participate in any feelings or policies of hate and vindictiveness. In describing Lincoln as throwing up his hands in the manner of scaring sheep, Secretary Welles quoted Lincoln as saying:

Frighten them out of the country, let down the bars, scare them off! Enough lives have been sacrificed. We must extinguish our resentment if we expect harmony and union.

Abraham Lincoln perceived the people of the former Confederacy as defeated, destroyed, desolate, and humiliated. The only feelings that he could hold were feelings of compassion, forgiveness, and amnesty.

Late in the afternoon the president and his wife took a carriage ride. Later, Mrs. Lincoln recalled how happy he had been by talking about the future years of peace in the White House before they returned to Illinois. After the carriage ride, the president met with Governor Oglesby of Illinois and other visitors.

For the evening of that fateful day, the president had promised to take his wife to Ford's Theater to see Laura Keen's performance of the stage play *Our American Cousin*. But the president was late for dinner, and after dinner he was delayed further by communications with the War Department.

Finally, the day's work was done. The President was extremely tired, but he was happy. At 8:30 P.M. on that notable day, Good Friday, April 14, 1865, Abraham Lincoln and his wife Mary departed from the White House in the presidential carriage to go to the theater.

The fifth of the Lincoln-Douglas debates was held on October 7, 1858 at Knox College, Galesburg, Illinois. The above artist's concept of the debate very accurately represents all historical accounts of the arrangements and circumstances of the debate. *Courtesy of the Illinois State Historical Library, Old State Capital, Springfield, Illinois.*

Selected Speeches from Abraham Lincoln

From the hundreds of public speeches, proclamations, and letters of President Lincoln, ten are presented here (some of them in a shortened form) for study and evaluation. The ten were chosen mainly because they represent best the development of Lincoln's clarity of thinking and style of expression on the major issues of his lifetime. The ten are:

1. Address Before the Young Men's Lyceum of Springfield, Illinois...............January 27, 1838
2. House Divided Speech Springfield................................June 16, 1858
3. Lincoln-Douglas Debate Alton...................................... October 15,1858
4. Cooper Union Address, New York City................. February 27, 1860
5. Farewell Address Springfield........................ February 11, 1861
6. Emancipation Proclamation ....January 1, 1863
7. Gettysburg Address............................ November 19, 1863
8. Proclamation of Amnesty .... December 8, 1863
9. Second Inaugural Address....................March 7, 1865
10. Last Public Address .... April 11, 1865

The "Old State Capitol" in Springfield served as the center of state government in Illinois for 1838 to 1878. Abraham Lincoln served his fourth term in the Illinois House of Representatives in this building during 1838-39. In the same House chamber he delivered his famous "House Divided Speech" in 1858 when accepting the nomination of his party to oppose Stephen A. Douglas for the U.S. Senate. In 1865 Lincoln's body lay in state in the House Chamber prior to his burial in Oakridge Cemetry. This photograph was taken in 1860 by R. H. Dawson. *Courtesy of the Illinois State Historical Library, Old State Capitol, Springfield, Illinois.*

**Address Before the Young Men's
Lyceum of Springfield, Illinois
January 27, 1838**

THE PERPETUATION OF OUR POLITICAL INSTITUTIONS

As a subject for the remarks of the evening, the perpetuation of our political institutions , is selected.

In the great journal of things happening under the sun, we, the American people, find our account running, under date of the nineteenth century of the Christian era. We find ourselves in the peaceful possession, of the fairest portion of the earth, as regards extent of territory, fertility of soil, and salubrity of climate. We find ourselves under the government of a system of political institutions, conducive more essentially to the ends of civil and religious liberty, than any of which the history of former times tells us. We, when mounting the stage of existence, found ourselves the legal inheritors of these fundamental blessings. We toiled not in the acquirement or establishment of them—they are a legacy bequeathed us, by a once hardy, brave and patriotic, but now lamented and departed, race of ancestors. Theirs was the task. . . . to possess themselves, and through themselves, us, of this goodly land; . . . ., tis ours only to transmit these, the former, unprofaned by the foot of an invader.

How, then, shall we perform it? At what point shall we expect danger? By what means shall we fortify against it? Shall we expect some trans-atlantic military giant to step the ocean and crush us at a blow? Never!

At what point then is the approach of danger to be expected? I answer, if it ever reach us, it must spring up amongst us. It cannot come from abroad. If destruction be our lot, we must ourselves be its author and finisher. As a nation of freemen, we must live through all time, or die by suicide.

I hope I am over wary; but if I am not, there is, even now, something of ill omen amongst us. I mean the increasing disregard for law which pervades the country; the growing disposition to substitute the passions in lieu of the sober judgment of the Courts; . . .

Accounts of outrages committed by mobs, form the everyday news of the times. . . . Those happening in the State of Mississippi, and at St. Louis, are, perhaps, the most dangerous in example. In the Mississippi case, they first commenced by hanging the regular gamblers:. . . . next, negroes, suspected of conspiring to raise an insurrection, were caught up and hanged in all parts of the State: then, white men, supposed to be leagued with the negroes: and finally, strangers, from neighboring States, going thither on business, were, in many instances, subjected to the same fate. Thus went on this process of hanging,. . . .

Turn, then, to that horror-striking scene at St. Louis. A single victim only was sacrificed there. His story is very short;. . . . A mulatto man, by the name of McIntosh, was seized in the street, dragged to the suburbs of the city, chained to a tree, and actually burned to death; . . . .

Such are the effects of mob law; and such are the scenes becoming more and more frequent in this land so lately famed for love of law and order; . . . .

The question recurs "how shall we fortify against it?" The answer is simple. Let every American, every lover of liberty, every wellwisher to his posterity, swear by the blood of the Revolution, never to violate in the least particular, the laws of the country; and never to tolerate their violation by others. As the patriots of seventy-six did to the support of the Declaration of Independence, so to the support of the Constitution and Laws, let every American pledge his life, his property, and his sacred honor; — let every man remember that to violate the law, is to trample on the blood of his father, ... Let reverence for the laws be breathed by every American mother, to the lisping babe, that prattles on her lap—let it be taught in schools, in seminaries, and in colleges;—let it be written in Primers, spelling books, and in Almanacs;—let it be preached from the pulpit, proclaimed in legislative halls, and enforced in courts of justice. And, in short, let it become the political religion of the nation;

. . . . Passion has helped us; but can do so no more. It will in future be our enemy. Reason, cold, calculating, unimpassioned reason, must furnish all the materials for our future support and defense. Let those materials be moulded into general intelligence, sound morality, and a reverence for the Constitution and Laws;. . . .

Upon these let the proud fabric of freedom rest; and as truly as has been said of the only greater institution, "the gates of hell shall not prevail against it."

Speech at Springfield, Illinois, June 16, 1858

A HOUSE DIVIDED

Mr. President and Gentlemen of the Convention:

If we could first know where we are, and whither we are tending, we could then better judge what to do, and how to do it.

We are now far into the fifth year, since a policy was initiated, with the avowed object, and confident promise, of putting an end to slavery agitation.

Under the operation of that policy, that agitation has not only not ceased, but has constantly augmented. In my opinion it will not cease, until a crisis shall have been reached and passed.

A house divided against itself cannot stand.

I believe this government cannot endure, permanently half slave and half free.

I do not expect the Union to be dissolved—I do not expect the house to fall—but I do expect it will cease to be divided. It will become all one thing or the other.

Either the opponents of slavery will arrest the further spread of it, and place it where the public mind shall rest in the belief that it is in course of ultimate extinction; or its advocates will push it forward till it shall become alike lawful in all the States, old as well as new—North as well as South.

Have we no tendency to the latter condition? . . . The new year of 1854 found slavery excluded from more than half the States by State Constitutions, and from most of the national territory by

Congressional prohibition. Four days later commenced the struggle which ended in repealing that Congressional prohibition. This opened all the national territory to slavery; and was the first point gained.

This necessity had not been overlooked; but had been provided for in the notable argument of "squatter sovereignty," otherwise called "sacred right of self-government," which latter phrase was so perverted in this attempted use of it as to amount to just this: That if any one man chose to enslave another, no third man shall be allowed to object.

That argument was incorporated into the Nebraska Bill itself, in the language which follows: "It being the true intent and meaning of this act not to legislate slavery into any Territory or State, not exclude it therefrom: but to leave the people thereof perfectly free to form and regulate their domestic institutions in their own way, subject only to the Constitution of the United States." Then opened the roar of loose declamation in favor of "Squatter Sovereignty," and "Sacred right of self-government."

"But," said the opposition members, "let us be more specific—let us amend the bill so as to expressly declare that the people of a territory may exclude slavery," "Not we," said the friends of the measure; and down they voted the amendment.

While the Nebraska bill was passing through Congress, a Law Case, involving the question of a negro's freedom, by reason of his owner having voluntarily taken him first into a free state and then into a territory covered by the Congressional prohibition, and held him as a slave, for a long time in each, was passing through the U.S. Circuit Court for the District of Missouri; and both Nebraska bill and law suit were brought to a decision in the same month of May, 1854. The negro's name was "Dred Scott," which name now designates the decision finally made in the case.

Before the then next Presidential election, the law case came to, and was argued in, the Supreme Court of the United States, but the decision of it was deferred until after the election. Still, before the election, Senator Trumbull, on the floor of the Senate, requests the leading advocate of the Nebraska bill to state his opinion whether the people of a territory can Constitutionally exclude slavery from their limits; and the latter answers, "That is a question for the Supreme Court."

The election came. Mr. Buchanan was elected, and the endorsement, such as it was, secured. That was the second point gained. The endorsement, however, fell short of a clear popular majority by nearly four hundred thousand votes, and so, perhaps, was not overwhelmingly reliable and satisfactory. The outgoing President, in his last annual message, as impressively as possible, echoed back upon the people the weight and authority of the endorsement.

The Supreme Court met again; did not announce their decision, but ordered a re-argument.

The Presidential inauguration came, and still no decision of the Supreme Court; but the incoming

President, in his inaugural address, fervently exhorted the people to abide by the forthcoming decision, whatever it might be. Then, in a few days, came the decision.

The reputed author of the Nebraska bill finds an early occasion to make a speech at this capitol endorsing this Dred Scott Decision, and vehemently denouncing all opposition to it.

The President, too, seizes the early occasion of the Silliman letter to endorse and strongly construe that decision, and to express his astonishment that any different view had ever been entertained.

At length a squabble springs up between the President and the author of the Nebraska bill, on the mere question of fact, whether the Lecompton Constitution was or was not, in any just sense, made by the people of Kansas; and in that squabble the latter declares that all he wants is a fair vote for the people, and that he cares not whether slavery be voted down or voted up.

And well may he cling to that principle. . . . That principle is the only shred left of his original Nebraska doctrine. Under the Dred Scott Decision, "squatter sovereignty" squatted out of existence, tumbled down like temporary scaffolding—like the mould at the foundry served through one blast and fell back into loose sand—helped to carry an election, and then was kicked to the winds. . . .

The several points of the Dred Scott Decision, in connection with Senator Douglas's "care not" policy, constitute the piece of machinery in its present state of advancement. This was the third point gained. The working points of that machinery are:

First that no negro slave, imported as such from Africa, and no descendant of such slave can ever be a citizen of any State, in the sense of that term as used in the Constitution of the United States. This point is made in order to deprive the negro, in every possible event, of the benefit of this provision of the United States Constitution, which declares that— "The citizens of each State shall be entitled to all privileges and immunities of citizens in the several States."

Secondly, that "subject to the Constitution of the United States," neither Congress nor a Territorial Legislature can exclude slavery from any United States territory. This point is made in order that individual men may fill up the territories with slaves, without danger of losing them as property, and thus to enhance the chances of permanency to the institution through all the future.

Thirdly, that whether the holding a negro in actual slavery in a free State makes him free, as against the holder, the United States courts will not decide, but will leave to be decided by the courts of any slave State the negro may be forced into by the master. This point is made, not to be pressed immediately; but, if acquiesced in for a while, and apparently endorsed by the people at an election, then to sustain the logical conclusion that what Dred Scott's master might lawfully do with Dred Scott, in the free State of Illinois, every other master may lawfully do with any other one, or a thousand slaves in Illinois, or in any other free state.

Auxiliary to all this, and working hand in hand with it, the Nebraska doctrine, or what is left of it, is to educate and mould public opinion, at least Northern public opinion, to not care whether slavery is voted down or voted up. This shows exactly where we now are; and partially also, whither we are tending.

It will throw additional light on the latter to go back and run the mind over the string of historical facts already stated. Several things will now appear less dark and mysterious than they did when they were transpiring. The people were to be left "perfectly free"—"subject only to the Constitution." What the Constitution had to do with it, outsiders could not then see. Plainly enough now, it was an exactly fitted niche for the Dred Scott Decision to afterwards come in and declare the perfect freedom of the people to be just no freedom at all.

Why was the amendment, expressly declaring the right of the people to exclude slavery, voted down? Plainly enough now, the adoption of it would have spoiled the niche for the Dred Scott Decision.

Why was the court decision held up? Why even a Senator's individual opinion withheld till after the Presidential election? Plainly enough now, the speaking out then would have damaged the "perfectly free" argument upon which the election was to be carried.

Why the outgoing President's felicitation on the endorsement? Why the delay of a reargument? Why the incoming President's advance exhortation in favor of the decision? These things look like the cautious patting and petting of spirited horse, preparatory to mounting him, when it is dreaded that he may give a rider a fall.

And why the hasty after endorsements of the decision by the President and others?

We can not absolutely know that all these exact adaptations are the result of preconcert. But when we see a lot of framed timbers, different portions of which we know have been gotten out at different times and places and by different workmen—Stephen, Franklin, Roger and James for instance—and when we see these timbers joined together, and see they exactly make the frame of a house or a mill, all the tenons and mortises exactly fitting, and all the lengths and proportions of the different pieces exactly adapted to their respective places, and not a piece too many or too few—not omitting even scaffolding—or, if a single piece be lacking, we can see the place in the frame exactly fitted and prepared to yet bring such piece in—in such case, we find it impossible to not believe that Stephen and Franklin and Roger and James all understood one another from the beginning, and all worked upon a common plan or draft drawn up before the first lick was struck.

It should not be overlooked that, by the Nebraska bill, the people of a State as well as Territory, were to be left "perfectly free" "subject only to the Constitution."

Why mention a State? They were legislating for territories, and not for or about States. Certainly the people of a State are and ought to be subject to the Constitution of the United States; but why is mention of this lugged into this merely territorial law? Why are the people of a territory and the people of a state therein lumped together, and their relation to the Constitution therein treated as being precisely the same?

While the opinion of the Court by Chief Justice Taney, in the Dred Scott case, and the separate opinions of all the concurring Judges, expressly declare that the Constitution of the United States neither permits Congress nor a Territorial legislature to exclude slavery from any United States territory, they all omit to declare whether or not the same Constitution permits a state, or the people of a State, to exclude it.

In what cases the power of the States is so restrained by the U.S. Constitution, is left an open question, precisely as the same question, as to the restraint on the power of the territories was left open in the Nebraska act. Put that and that together, and we have another nice little niche, which we may, ere long, see filled with another Supreme Court Decision declaring that the Constitution of the United States does not permit a State to exclude slavery from its limits.

And this may especially be expected if the doctrine of "care not whether slavery be voted DOWN or voted UP," shall gain upon the public mind sufficiently to give promise that such a decision can be maintained when made: Such a decision is all that slavery now lacks of being alike lawful in all the States.

Welcome or unwelcome, such decision is probably coming, and will soon be upon us, unless the power of the present political dynasty shall be met and overthrown.

We shall lie down pleasantly dreaming that the people of Missouri are on the verge of making their State free; and we shall awake to the reality, instead, that the Supreme Court has made Illinois a slave State. To meet and overthrow the power of that dynasty, is the work now before all those who would prevent that consummation.

That is what we have to do. But how can we best do it?

There are those who denounce us openly to their own friends, yet whisper to us softly, that Senator Douglas is the aptest instrument there is, with which to effect that object. They do not tell us, nor has he told us, that he wishes any such object to be effected. They wish us to infer all, from the facts, that he now has a little quarrel with the present head of the dynasty; and that he has regularly voted with us, on a single point, upon which he and we have never differed.

They remind us that he is a very great man, and that the largest of us are very small ones. Let this be granted. But "a living dog is better than a dead lion." Judge Douglas, if not a dead lion for this work, is at least a caged and toothless one. How can he oppose the advances of slavery? He don't care anything about it. His avowed mission is impressing the "public heart" to care nothing about it.

Two years ago the Republicans of the nation mustered over thirteen hundred thousand strong. We did this under the single impulse of resistance to a common danger.

Did we brave all then, to falter now?—now—when that same enemy is wavering, dissevered and belligerent? The result is not doubtful. We shall not fail—if we stand firm, we shall not fail.

Wise councils may accelerate or mistakes delay it, but sooner or later the victory is sure to come.

Seventh and Last Debate Between Abraham Lincoln and Stephen A. Douglas at Alton, Illinois October 15, 1853

MR. LINCOLN'S REPLY

Ladies and Gentlemen: — I have been somewhat, in my own mind, complimented by a large portion of Judge Douglas's speech—I mean that portion which he devotes to the controversy between himself and the present Administration. [cheers and laughter] This is the seventh time Judge Douglas and myself have met in these joint discussions, and he has been gradually improving in regard to his war with the Administration. [laughter] At Quincy, day before yesterday, he was a little more severe upon the Administration than I had heard him upon any former occasion, and I took pains to compliment him for it. I then told him to "Give it to them" with all the power he had; and as some of them were present I told them I would be very much obliged if they would give it to him in about the same way. . . . [uproarious laughter and cheers]

There is one other thing I will mention before I leave this branch of the discussion. . . . I refer to that branch of the Judge's remarks where he undertakes to involve Mr. Buchanan in an inconsistency. He reads something from Buchanan, from which he undertakes to involve him in an inconsistency; and he gets something of a cheer for having done so. I would only remind the Judge that while he is very valiantly fighting for the Nebraska bill and the repeal of the Missouri Compromise, it has been but a little while since he was the valiant advocate of the Missouri Compromise. [cheers] I want to know if Buchanan has not as much right to be inconsistent as Douglas has? [applause and laughter] Has Douglas the exclusive right, in this country, of being on all sides of all questions? [great laughter]

I have stated upon former occasions, and I may as well state again, what I understand to be the real issue in the controversy between Judge Douglas and myself. On the point of my wanting to make war between the free and the slave States, there has been no issue between us. So, too, when he assumes that I am in favor of introducing a perfect social and political equality between the white and black races. These are false issues, upon which Judge Douglas has tried to force the controversy. There is no foundation in truth for the charge that I maintain either of these propositions.

The real issue in this controversy—the one pressing upon every mind—is the sentiment on the part of one class that looks upon the institution of slavery as a wrong, and of another class that does not look upon it as a wrong. The sentiment that contemplates the institution of slavery in this country as a wrong is the sentiment of the Republican party. It is the sentiment around which all their actions—all their arguments circle—from which all their propositions radiate. They look upon it as being a moral, social and political wrong; and while they contemplate it as such, they nevertheless have due regard for its actual existence among us, and the difficulty of getting rid of it in any satisfactory way, and to all the constitutional obligations thrown about it. Yet having a due regard for these, they desire a policy in regard to it that looks to its not creating any more danger. They insist that it should be treated as a wrong, and one of the methods of treating it as a wrong is to make provision that it shall grow no larger. . . . [loud applause]

On this subject of treating it as a wrong, and limiting its spread, let me say a word. Has anything ever threatened the existence of this Union save and except this very institution of Slavery? What is it that we hold most dear amongst us? Our own liberty and prosperity. What has ever threatened our liberty and prosperity save and except this institution of Slavery? If this is true, how do you propose to improve the condition of things by enlarging Slavery—by spreading it out and making it bigger? You may have a wen or a cancer upon your person and not be able to cut it out lest you bleed to death; but surely it is no way to cure it, to engraft it and spread it over your whole body. That is no proper way of treating what you regard as a wrong. . . .

On the other hand, I have said there is a sentiment which treats it as not being wrong. That is the Democratic sentiment of this day. I do not mean to say that every man who stands within that range positively asserts that it is right. That class will include all who positively assert that it is right, and all who like Judge Douglas treat it as indifferent and do not say it is either right or wrong. These two classes of men fall within the general class of those who do not look upon it as a wrong. . . .

The Democratic policy in regard to that institution will not tolerate the merest breath, the slightest hint, of the least degree of wrong about it. Try it by some of Judge Douglas's arguments. He says he "don't care whether it is voted up or voted down" in the territories.

Any man can say that who does not see anything wrong in slavery, but no man can logically say it who does see a wrong in it; because no man can logically say he don't care whether a wrong is voted up or voted down. He may say he don't care whether an indifferent thing is voted up or down, but he must logically have a choice between a right thing and a wrong thing. He contends that whatever community wants slaves has a right to have them. So they have, if it is not a wrong. But if it is a wrong, he cannot say people have a right to do wrong.

He says that upon the score of equality, slaves should be allowed to go in a new Territory, like other property. This is strictly logical if there is no difference between it and other property. If it and other property are equal, his argument is entirely logical. But if you insist that one is wrong and the other right, there is no use to institute a comparison between right and wrong. . . .

That is the real issue. That is the issue that will continue in this country when these poor tongues of Judge Douglas and myself shall be silent. It is the eternal struggle between these two principles—right and wrong—throughout the world. They are the two principles that have stood face to face from the beginning of time; and will ever continue to struggle. The one is the common right of humanity and the other the divine right of kings. It is the same principle in whatever shape it develops itself. It is the same spirit that says, "You work and toil and earn bread, and I'll eat it." [applause] No matter in what shape it comes, whether from the mouth of a king who seeks to bestride the people of his own nation and live by the fruit of their labor, or from one race of men as an apology for enslaving another race, it is the same tyrannical principle. . . .

I understand I have ten minutes yet. I will employ it in saying something about this Dred Scott Decision, that the people of the Territories can still somehow exclude slavery. The first thing I ask attention to is the fact that Judge Douglas constantly said, before the decision, that whether they could or not, was a question for the Supreme Court. [cheers] But after the Court has made the decision, he virtually says it is NOT a question for the Supreme Court, but for the people. [applause] And how is it he tells us they can exclude it? He says it needs "police regulations," and that admits of "unfriendly legislation." Although is is a right established by the Constitution of the United States to take a slave into a Territory of the United States and hold him as property, yet unless the Territorial Legislature will give friendly legislation, and, more especially, if they adopt unfriendly legislation, they can practically exclude him.

Now, without meeting this proposition as a matter of fact, I pass to consider the real constitutional obligation. Let me take the gentleman who looks me in the face before me, and let us suppose that he is a member of the Territorial Legislature. The first thing he will do will be to swear that he will support the Constitution of the United States.

His neighbor by his side in the Territory has slaves and needs Territorial legislation to enable him to enjoy that constitutional right. Can he withhold the legislation which his neighbor needs for the enjoyment of a right which is fixed in his favor in the Constitution of the United States which he has sworn to support? Can he withhold it without violating his oath? And more especially, can he pass unfriendly legislation to violate his oath? Why this is a MONSTROUS sort of talk about the Constitution of the United States! [great applause] THERE HAS NEVER BEEN AS OUTLANDISH OR LAWLESS A DOCTRINE FROM THE MOUTH OF ANY RESPECTABLE MAN ON EARTH! [tremendous cheers]

I do not believe it is a Constitutional right to hold slaves in a Territory of the United States. I believe the decision was improperly made and I go for reversing it. Judge Douglas is furious against those who go for reversing a decision. But he is for legislating it out of all force while the law itself stands. I repeat that there has never been so monstrous a doctrine uttered from the mouth of a respectable man. . . . [cheers]

Address at Cooper Union Institute, New York City February 27, 1860

Mr. President and Fellow Citizens of New York: The facts with which I shall deal this evening are mainly old and familar; nor is there anything new in the general use I shall make of them. If there shall be any novelty, it will be in the mode of presenting the facts, and the inferences and observations following that presentation.

In his speech last autumn, at Columbus, Ohio, as reported in "The New York Times," Senator Douglas said:

"Our fathers, when they framed the Government under which we live, understood this question just as well, and even better, than we do now."

I fully endorse this, and I adopt it as a text for this discourse. I so adopt it because it furnishes a precise and an agreed starting point for a discussion between Republicans and that wing of the Democracy headed by Senator Douglas. It simply leaves the inquiry: "What was the understanding these fathers had of the question mentioned?"

What is the frame of Government under which we live?

The answer must be: "The Constitution of the United States." That Constitution consists of the original, framed in 1787, (and under which the present government first went into operation,) and twelve subsequently framed amendments, the first ten of which were framed in 1789.

Who were our fathers that framed the Constitution? I suppose the "Thirty-nine" who signed the original instrument may be fairly called our fathers who framed that part of the present Government. . . .

I take these "Thirty-nine" for the present, as being "our fathers who framed the Government under which we live."

What is the question which, according to the text, those fathers understood "just as well, and even better than we do now?"

It is this: Does the proper division of local from federal authority, or anything in the Constitution, forbid our Federal Government to control as to slavery in our Federal Territories?

Upon this, Senator Douglas holds the affirmative, and Republicans the negative. This affirmation and denial form an issue; and this issue—this question—is precisely what the text declares our fathers understood "better than we."

Let us now inquire whether the "Thirty-nine," or any of them, ever acted upon this question; and if they did, how they acted upon it—how they expressed that better understanding?

In 1784, three years before the Constitution—the United States then owning the Northwestern Territory, and no other, the Congress of the Confederation had before them the question of prohibiting slavery in that Territory; and four of the "Thirty-nine," who afterward framed the Constitution, were in that Congress, and voted on that question. Of these, Roger Sherman, Thomas Mifflin, and Hugh Williamson voted for the prohibition, thus showing that, in their understanding, no line dividing local from federal authority, nor anything else, properly forbade the Federal Government to control as to slavery in federal territory. The other of the four—James M. Henry—voted against the prohibition, showing that, for some cause, he thought it improper to vote for it.

In 1787, still before the Constitution, but while the Convention was in session framing it, and while the Northwestern Territory still was the only territory owned by the United States, the same question of prohibiting slavery in the territory again came before the Congress of the Confederation; and two more of the "Thirty-nine" who afterward signed the

Constitution, were in that Congress, and voted on the question. They were William Blount and William Few, and they both voted for the prohibition—thus showing that, in their understanding, no line dividing local from federal authority, nor anything else, properly forbade the Federal Government to control as to slavery in federal territory. This time the prohibition became a law, being part of what is now well-known as the Ordinance of '87.

The question of federal control of slavery in the territories, seems not to have been directly before the Convention which framed the original Constitution; and hence it is not recorded that the "Thirty-nine," or any of them, while engaged on that instrument, expressed any opinion of that precise question. In 1789, by the first congress which sat under the Constitution, an act was passed to enforce the Ordinance of '87, including the prohibition of slavery in the Northwestern Territory. The bill for this act was reported by one of the "Thirty-nine," Thomas Fitzsimmons, then a member of the House of Representatives from Pennsylvania. It went through all its stages without a worrd of opposition, and finally passed both branches without yeas and nays, which is equivalent to an unanimous passage. In this Congress there were sixteen of the thirty-nine fathers who framed the original Constitution. They were John Langdon, Nicholas Gilman, William S. Johnson, Roger Sherman, Robert Morris, Thomas Fitzsimmons, William Few, Abraham Baldwin, Rufus King, William Paterson, George Clymer, Richard Bassett, George Read, Pierce Butler, Daniel Carroll, James Madison.

This shows that, in their understanding, no line dividing local from federal authority, nor anything in the Constitution, properly forbade Congress to prohibit slavery in the federal territory; else both their fidelity to correct principle, and their oath to support the Constitution, would have constrained them to oppose the prohibition.

Again, George Washington, another of the "Thirty-nine," was then President of the United States, and, as such, approved and signed the bill; thus completing its validity as a law, and thus showing that, in his understanding, no line dividing local from federal authority, nor anything in the Constitution, forbade the Federal Government, to control as to slavery in federal territory.

No great while after the adoption of the original Constitution, North Carolina ceded to the Federal Government the country now constituting the State of Tennessee; and a few years later Georgia ceded that which now constitutes the States of Mississippi and Alabama. In both deeds of cession it was made a condition by the ceding States that the Federal Government should not prohibit slavery in the ceded country. Besides this, slavery was then actually in the ceded country. Under these circumstances, Congress, on taking charge of these countries, did not absolutely prohibit slavery within them. But they did interfere with it—take control of it—even there, to a certain extent. In 1789, Congress organized the Territory of Mississippi. In the act of organization, they prohibited the bringing of slaves into the Territory, from any place without the United States, by fine, and giving freedom to slaves so brought. This act passed both branches of Congress without yeas and nays.

In that Congress were three of the "Thirty-nine" who framed the original Constitution. They were John Langdon, George Read and Abraham Baldwin. They all, probably, voted for it. Certainly they would have placed their opposition to it upon record, if, in their understanding, any line dividing local from federal authority, or anything in the Constitution, properly forbade the Federal Government to control as to slavery in federal territory.

In 1803, the Federal Government purchased the Louisiana country. Our former territorial acquisition came from certain of our own States; but this Louisiana country was acquired from a foreign nation. In 1804, Congress gave a territorial organization to that part of it which now constitutes the State of Louisiana. New Orleans, lying within that part, was an old and comparatively large city. There were other considerable towns and settlements, and slavery was extensively and thoroughly inter-mingled with the people. Congress did not, in the Territorial Act, prohibit slavery; but they did inter-fere with it—take control of it—in a more marked extensive way than they did in the case of Missis-sippi. The substance of the provision therein made, in relation to slaves was:

First. That no slave should be imported into the territory from foreign parts.

Second. That no slave should be carried into it who had been imported into the U.S. since the first day of May, 1798.

Third. That no slave should be carried into it, except by the owner, and for his own use as a settler; the penalty in all cases being a fine upon the violator of the law, and freedom to the slave.

This act also was passed without yeas and nays. In the Congress which passed it, there were two of the "Thirty-nine." They were Abraham Baldwin and Jonathan Dayton. As stated in the case of Missis-sippi, it is probable they both voted for it. They would not have allowed it to pass without record-ing their opposition to it, if, in their understanding, it violated either the line properly dividing local from federal authority, or any provision of the Constitution.

In 1819-20, came and passed the Missouri ques-tion. Many votes were taken, by yeas and nays, in both branches of Congress, upon the various phases of the general question. Two of the "Thirty-nine"—Rufus King and Charles Pinckney—were members of that Congress. Mr. King steadily voted for slavery prohibition and against all compromises, while Mr. Pinckney as steadily voted against slavery prohibi-tion and against all compromises. . . .

The cases I have mentioned are the only acts of the "Thirty-nine," or of any of them, upon the direct issue, which I have been able to discover.

To enumerate the persons who thus acted, as being four in 1784, two in 1787, seventeen in 1789, three in 1798, two in 1804, and two in 1819-20—there would be thirty of them. But this would be counting John Langdon, Roger Sherman, William Few, Rufus King, and George Read, each twice; and Abraham Baldwin three times. The true number of those of the "Thirty-nine" whom I have shown to have acted upon the question, which, by the text, they under-stood better than we, is twenty-three, leaving six-teen not shown to have acted upon it in any way.

Here, then, we have twenty-three out of our

thirty-nine fathers "who framed the Government under which we live," who have, upon their official responsibility and their corporal oaths, acted upon the very question which the text affirms they "understood just as well, and even better than we do now," and twenty-one of them—a clear majority of the whole "thirty-nine"—so acting upon it as to make them guilty of gross political impropriety and willful perjury, if, in their understanding, any proper division between local and federal authority, or anything in the Constitution they had made themselves, and sworn to support, forbade the Federal Government to control as to slavery in the federal territories. Thus the twenty-one acted; and, as actions speak louder than words, so actions, under such responsibility, speak still louder. . . .

But enough! Let all who believe that "our fathers, who framed the Government under which we live, understood this question just as well, and even better, than we do now," speak as they spoke and act as they acted upon it. This is all Republicans ask—all Republicans desire—in relation to slavery. As those fathers marked it, so let it be again marked, as an evil not to be extended, but to be tolerated and protected only because of and so far as its actual presence among us makes that toleration and protection a necessity. Let all the guarantees those fathers gave it, be, not grudgingly, but fully and fairly maintained. For this Republicans contend, and with this, so far as I know or believe, they will be content.

And now, ... I would address a few words to the Southern people.

I would say to them;—You consider yourselves a reasonable and a just people; and I consider that in the general qualities of reason and justice you are not inferior to any other people. Still, when you speak of us Republicans, you do so only to denounce us as reptiles, or, at best, as no better than outlaws. You will grant a hearing to pirates or murderers, but nothing like it to "Black Republicans." In all your contentions with one another, each of you deems an unconditional condemnation of "Black Republicanism" as the first thing to be attended to. . . .

But you say you are conservative—eminently conservative—while we are revolutionary, destructive, or something of the sort. What is conservatism? Is it not adherence to the old and tried, against the new and untried? We stick to, contend for, the identical old policy on the point in controversy which was adopted by "our fathers who framed the Government under which we live;" while you. . . . insist upon something new. True, you disagree among yourselves as to what that substitute shall be. You are divided on new propositions and plans, but you are unanimous in rejecting the old policy of the fathers. Some of you are for reviving the foreign slave trade; some for a Congressional Slave-Code for the Territories; some for Congress forbidding the Territories to prohibit Slavery within their limits; some for maintaining Slavery in the Territories through the judiciary; some for the "gur-reat purrinciple" that "if one man would enslave another, no third man should object," fantastically called "Popular Sovereignty;" but never a man among you in favor of federal prohibition of slavery in federal territories, according to the practice of "our fathers who framed the Government under which we live. . . ."

Again, you say we have made the slavery question more prominent than it formerly was. We deny it. We admit that it is more prominent, but we deny that we made it so. It was not we, but you, who discarded the old policy of our fathers. We resisted, and still resist, your innovation; and thence comes the greater prominence of the question. Would you have that question reduced to its former proportions? Go back to that old policy. What has been will be again, under the same conditions. If you would have the peace of the old times, readopt the precepts and policy of the old times.

You charge that we stir up insurrections among your slaves. We deny it; and what is your proof? Harpers Ferry! John Brown! John Brown was no Republican; and you have failed to implicate a single Republican in his Harpers Ferry enterprise. If any member of our party is guilty in that matter, you know it or you do not know it. If you do know it, you are inexcusable for not designating the man and proving the fact. If you do not know it, you are inexcusable for asserting it, and especially for persisting in the assertion after you have tried and failed to make the proof. You need not be told that persisting in a charge which one does not know to be true, is simply malicious slander. . . .

In the language of Mr. Jefferson, uttered many years ago, "It is still in our power to direct the process of emancipation, and deportation, peaceable, and in such slow degrees, as that the evil will wear off insensibly; and their places, be "pari passu," filled up by free white laborers. If, on the contrary, it is left to force itself on, human nature must shudder at the prospect held up."

Mr. Jefferson did not mean to say, nor do I, that the power of emancipation is in the Federal Government. He spoke of Virginia; and, as to the power of emancipation, I speak of the slaveholding States only. The Federal Government, however, as we insist, has the power of restraining the extension of the institution. . . .

A few words now to Republicans. It is exceedingly desirable that all parts of this great Confederacy shall be at peace, and in harmony, one with another. Let us Republicans do our part to have it so. Even though much provoked, let us do nothing through passion and ill temper. Even though the Southern people will not so much as listen to us, let us calmly consider their demands, and yield to them if, in our deliberate view of our duty, we possibly can. Judging by all they say and do, and by the subject and nature of their controversy with us, let us determine, if we can, what will satisfy them.

Will they be satisfied if the Territories be unconditionally surrendered to them? We know they will not. In all their present complaints against us, the Territories are scarcely mentioned. Invasions and insurrections are the rage now. Will it satisfy them, if, in the future, we have nothing to do with invasions and insurrections? We know it will not. . . .

The question recurs, what will satisfy them? Simply this: We must not only let them alone, but we must, somehow, convince them that we do let them alone. . . .

I am also aware they have not, as yet, in terms, demanded the overthrow of our Free-State Constitutions. Yet those Constitutions declare the wrong of slavery, with more solemn emphasis, than do all other sayings against it; and when all these other sayings shall have been silenced, the overthrow of these Constitutions will be demanded, and nothing be left to resist the demand. . . . Demanding what they do, and for the reason they do, they can voluntarily stop nowhere short of this consummation. Holding, as they do, that slavery is morally right, and socially elevating, they cannot cease to demand a full national recognition of it, as a legal right, and a social blessing.

Nor can we justifiably withold this, on any ground save our conviction that slavery is wrong. If slavery is right, all words, acts, laws, and constitutions against it, are themselves wrong, and should be silenced, and swept away. If it is right, we cannot justly object to its nationality—its universality: if it is wrong, they cannot justly insist upon its extension—its enlargement. All they ask, we could readily grant, if we thought slavery right; all we ask, they could as readily grant, if they thought it wrong. Their thinking it right, and our thinking it wrong, is the precise fact upon which depends the whole controversy. Thinking it right; as they do, they are not to blame for desiring its full recognition, as being right; but, thinking it wrong, as we do, can we yield to them? Can we cast our votes with their view, and against our own? In view of our moral, social, and political responsibilities, can we do this?

Wrong as we think slavery is, we can yet afford to let it alone where it is, because that much is due to the necessity arising from its actual presence in the nation; but can we, while our votes will prevent it, allow it to spread into the National Territories, and to overrun us here in these Free States? If our sense of duty forbids this, then let us stand by our duty, fearlessly and effectively. Let us be diverted by none of those sophistical contrivances wherewith we are so industriously plied and belabored—contrivances such as groping for some middle ground between the right and the wrong, vain as the search for a man who should be neither a living man nor a dead man—such as a policy of "don't care" on a question about which all true men do care—such as Union appeals beseeching true Union men to yield to Disunionists, reversing the divine rule, and calling, not the sinners, but the righteous to repentance—such as invocations to Washington, imploring men to unsay what Washington said, and undo what Washington did.

Neither let us be slandered from our duty by false accusations against us, nor frightened from it by menaces of destruction to the Government nor of dungeons to ourselves. Let us have faith that right makes might, and in that faith, let us, to the end, dare to do our duty as we understand it.

Farewell Address—Springfield, Illinois
February 11, 1861

My friends—No one, not in my situation, can appreciate my feeling of sadness at this parting. To this place, and the kindness of these people, I owe everything. Here I have lived a quarter of a century, and I have passed from a young to an old man. Here my children have been born, and one is buried. I now leave, not knowing when, or whether ever, I may return, with a task before me greater than that which rested upon Washington. Without the assistance of that Divine Being, who ever attended him, I cannot succeed. With that assistance I cannot fail. Trusting in Him, who can go with me, and remain with you and be everywhere for good, let us confidently hope that all will yet be well. To His care commending you, as I hope in your prayers you will commend me, I bid you an affectionate farewell.

Emancipation Proclamation
January 1, 1863

BY THE PRESIDENT OF THE UNITED STATES OF AMERICA
A PROCLAMATION

Whereas, on the twenty-second day of September, in the year of our Lord one thousand eight hundred and sixty-two, a proclamation was issued by the President of the United States, containing, among other things, the following, to wit:

That on the first day of January, in the year of our Lord one thousand eight hundred and sixty-three, all persons held as slaves within any State or designated part of a State, the people whereof shall then be in rebellion against the United States, shall be then, thenceforward, and forever free; and the Executive Government of the United States, including the military and naval authority thereof, will recognize and maintain the freedom of such persons, and will do no act or acts to repress such persons, or any of them, in any efforts they may make for their actual freedom.

That the Executive will, in the first day of January aforesaid, by proclamation, designate the States and parts of States, if any, in which the people thereof, respectively shall then be in rebellion against the United States; and the fact that any State, or the people thereof, shall on that day be, in good faith, represented in the Congress of the United States by members chosen thereto at elections wherein a majority of the qualified voters of such State shall have participated, shall, in the absence of strong countervailing testimony, be deemed conclusive evidence that such State, and the people thereof, are not then in rebellion against the United States.

Now, therefore, I, Abraham Lincoln, President of the United States, by virtue of the power in me vested as Commander-in-Chief, of the Army and Navy of the United States in time of actual armed rebellion against authority and government of the United States, and as a fit and necessary war measure for suppressing said rebellion, do on this first day of January, in the year of our Lord one thousand eight hundred and sixty-three, and in accordance with my purpose so to do publicly proclaimed for the full period of one hundred days, from the day first above mentioned, order and designate as the States and parts of States wherein the people thereof respectively, are this day in rebellion against the United States, the following, to wit:

Arkansas, Texas, Louisiana (except the Parishes of St. Bernard, Plaquemines, Jefferson, St. Johns, St. Charles, St. James, Ascension, Assumption, Terrebonne, Lafourche, St. Mary, St. Martin, and Orleans, including the City of New Orleans), Mississippi, Alabama, Florida, Georgia, South Carolina, North Carolina, and Virginia (except the forty-eight counties designated as West Virginia, and also the counties of Berkley, Accomac, Northampton, Elizabeth City, York, Princess Ann, and Norfolk, including the cities of Norfolk & Portsmouth); and which excepted parts are for the present, left precisely as if this proclamation were not issued.

And by virtue of the power, and for the purpose aforesaid, I do order and declare that all persons held as slaves within said designated States, and parts of States, are, and henceforward shall be free; and the Executive government of the United States, including the military and naval authorities thereof, will recognize and maintain the freedom of said persons.

And I hereby enjoin upon the people so declared to be free to abstain from all violence, unless in necessary self-defense; and I recommend to them that, in all cases when allowed, they labor faithfully for reasonable wages.

And I further declare and make known, that such persons of suitable condition, will be received into the armed service of the United States to garrison forts, positions, stations, and other places, and to man vessels of all sorts in said service.

And upon this act, sincerely believed to be an act of justice, warranted by the Constitution, upon military necessity, I invoke the considerate judgment of mankind, and the gracious favor of Almighty God.

In witness whereof, I have hereunto set my hand and caused the seal of the United States to be affixed.

Done at the City of Washington, this first day of January, in the year of our Lord one thousand eight hundred and sixty-three, and of the Independence of the United States of America the eighty-seventh.

By the President: Abraham Lincoln
William H. Seward, Secretary of State.

Address Delivered at the Dedication
of the Cemetery at Gettysburg
November 19, 1863

Four score and seven years ago our fathers brought forth on this continent, a new nation, conceived in Liberty, and dedicated to the proposition that all men are created equal.

Now we are engaged in a great civil war, testing whether that nation, or any nation so conceived and so dedicated, can long endure. We are met on a great battlefield of that war. We have come to dedicate a portion of that field, as a final resting place for those who here gave their lives that that nation might live. It is altogether fitting and proper that we should do this.

But, in a larger sense, we can not dedicate—we cannot consecrate—we cannot hallow—this ground. The brave men, living and dead, who struggled here, have consecrated it, far above our poor power to add or detract. The world will little note, nor long remember what we say here, but it can never forget what they did here. It is rather for us to be here dedicated to the great task remaining before us— that from these honored dead we take increased devotion—that we here highly resolve that these dead shall not have died in vain—that this nation, under God, shall have a new birth of freedom—and that government of the people, by the people, for the people, shall not perish from the earth.

Proclamation of Amnesty and Reconstruction
December 8, 1863

BY THE PRESIDENT OF THE
UNITED STATES OF AMERICA:
A PROCLAMATION

Whereas, in and by the Constitution of the United States, it is provided that the President "shall have power to grant reprieves and pardons for offenses against the United States, except in cases of impeachment;" and

Whereas, a rebellion now exists whereby the loyal State governments of several States have for a long time been subverted, and many persons have committed and are now guilty of treason against the United States; and

Whereas, with reference to said rebellion and treason, laws have been enacted by Congress declaring forfeitures and confiscation of property and liberation of slaves, all upon terms and conditions therein stated, and also declaring that the President was thereby authorized at any time thereafter, by proclamation, to extend to persons who may have participated in the existing rebellion, in any State or part thereof, pardon and amnesty, with such exceptions and at such times and on such conditions as he may deem expedient for the public welfare; and

Whereas, the Congressional declaration for limited and conditional pardon accords with well-established judicial exposition of the pardoning power; and

Whereas, with reference to said rebellion, the President of the United States has issued several proclamations, with provisions in regard to the liberation of slaves; and

Whereas, it is now desired by some persons heretofore engaged in said rebellion to resume their allegiance to the United States, and to reinaugurate loyal State governments within and for their respective States; therefore,

I, Abraham Lincoln, President of the United States, do proclaim, declare, and make known to all persons who have, directly or by implication, participated in the existing rebellion, except as hereinafter excepted, that a full pardon is hereby granted to them and each of them, with restoration of all rights of property, except as to slaves, and in property cases where rights of third parties shall have intervened, and upon the condition that every such person shall take and subscribe an oath, and thenceforward keep and maintain said oath inviolate; and which oath shall be registered for permanent preservation, and shall be of the tenor and effect following, to wit:

I, _____, do solemnly swear, in the presence of Almighty God, that I will henceforth faithfully support, protect and defend the Constitution of the United States, and the union of the States thereunder; and that I will, in like manner, abide by and faithfully support all acts of Congress passed during the existing rebellion with reference to slaves, so long and so far as not repealed, modified or held void by Congress, or by decision of the Supreme Court; and that I will, in like manner, abide by and faithfully support all proclamations of the President made during the existing rebellion having reference to slaves, so long and so far as not modified or declared void by decision of the Supreme Court. So help me God.

The persons excepted from the benefits of the foregoing provisions are all who are, or shall have been civil or diplomatic officers or agents of the so-called confederate government; all who have left judicial stations under the United States to aid the rebellion; all who are, or shall have been, military or naval officers of said so-called confederate government above the rank of colonel in the army, or of lieutenant in the navy; all who left seats in the United States Congress to aid the rebellion; all who

resigned commissions in the army or navy of the United States, and afterwards aided the rebellion; and all who have engaged in any way in treating colored persons or white persons, in charge of such, otherwise than lawfully as prisioners of war, and which persons may have been found in the United States service, as soldiers, seamen, or in any other capacity.

And I do further proclaim, declare, and make known, that whenever, in any of the States of Arkansas, Texas, Louisiana. Mississippi, Tennessee, Alabama, Georgia, Florida, South Carolina, and North Carolina, a number of persons not less than one-tenth in number of the votes cast in such State at the Presidential election of the year of our Lord one thousand eight hundred and sixty each having taken the oath aforesaid and not having since violated it, and being a qualified voter by the election law of the State existing immediately before the so-called act of secession, and excluding all others, shall re-establish a State government which shall be republican, and in no wise contravening said oath, such shall be recognized as the true government of the State, and the provision which declares that "The United States shall guaranty to every State in this union a republican form of government, and shall protect each of them against invasion; and, on application of the legislature, or the executive, (when the legislature cannot be convened,) against domestic violence".

And I do further proclaim, declare, and make known that any provision which may be adopted by such State government in relation to the freed people of such State, which shall recognize and declare their permanent freedom, provide for their education, and which may yet be consistent, as a temporary arrangement, with their present condition as a laboring, landless, and homeless class, will not be objected to by the national Executive. And it is suggested as not improper, that, in constructing a loyal State government in any State, the name of the State, the boundary, the subdivisions, the constitution, and the general code of laws, as before the rebellion, be maintained subject only to the modifications made necessary by the conditions herein before stated, and such others, if any, not contravening said conditions, and which may be deemed expedient by those framing the new State government.

To avoid misunderstanding, it may be proper to say that this proclamation, so far as it relates to State governments, has no reference to States wherein loyal State governments have all the while been maintained. And for the same reason, it may be proper to further say that whether members sent to Congress from any State shall be admitted to seats, constitutionally rests exclusively with the respective Houses, and not to any extent with the Executive. And still further, that this proclamation is intended to present the people of the States wherein the national authority has been suspended, and loyal State governments have been subverted, a mode in and by which the national authority and loyal State governments may be re-established within said States, or in any of them; and, while the mode presented is the best the Executive can suggest, with his present impressions, it must not be understood that no other possible mode, would be acceptable.

Given under my hand at the city of Washington, the 8th day of December, A.D., one thousand eight hundred and sixty-three, and of the independence of the United States of America the eighty-eight.
Abraham Lincoln

Second Inaugural Address
March 4, 1865

Fellow Countrymen:

At this second appearing to take the oath of the presidential office, there is less occasion for an extended address than there was at the first. Then a statement, somewhat in detail, of a course to be pursued, seemed fitting and proper. Now, at the expiration of four years, during which public declarations have been constantly called forth on every point and phase of the great contest which still absorbs the attention, and engrosses the energies of the nation, little that is new could be presented. The progress of our arms, upon which all else chiefly depends, is as well known to the public as to myself; and it is, I trust, reasonable satisfactory and encouraging to all. With high hope for the future, no prediction in regard to it is ventured.

On the occasion corresponding to this four years ago, all thoughts were anxiously directed to an impending civil war. All dreaded it—all sought to avert it. While the inaugural address was being delivered from this place, devoted altogether to saving the Union without war, insurgent agents were in the city seeking to destroy it without war—seeking to dissolve the Union, and divide effects, by negotiation. Both parties deprecated war; but one of them would make war rather than let the nation survive; and the other would accept war rather than let it perish. And the war came.

One-eighth of the whole population were colored slaves, not distributed generally over the Union, but localized in the Southern part of it. These slaves constituted a peculiar and powerful interest. All knew that this interest was, somehow, the cause of the war; while the government claimed no right to do more than to restrict the territorial enlargement of it. Neither party expected for the war, the magnitude, or the duration which it has already attained. Neither anticipated that the cause of the conflict might cease with, or even before, the conflict itself should cease. Each looked for an easier triumph, and a result less fundamental and astounding.

Both read the same Bible, and pray to the same God; and each invokes His aid against the other. It may seem strange that any men should dare to ask a just God's assistance in wringing their bread from the sweat of other men's faces; but let us judge not that we be not judged. The prayers of both could not be answered; that of neither has been answered fully. The Almighty has His own purposes. "Woe unto the world because of offences! For it must needs be that offences come; but woe to that man by whom the offence cometh!" If we shall suppose that American Slavery is one of those offences which, in the providence of God, must needs come, but which, having continued through His appointed time, He now wills to remove, and that He gives to both North and South, this terrible war, as the woe due to those by whom the offence came, shall we discern therein any departure from those divine attributes which the believers in the Living God always ascribe to Him? Fondly do we hope—fervently do we pray—that this mighty scourge of war may speedily pass away. Yet, if God wills that it continue, until all the wealth piled by the bond-man's two hundred and fifty years of unrequited toil shall be sunk, and until every drop of blood drawn with the lash, shall be paid by another drawn with the word, as was said three thousand years ago, so still it must be said "the judgments of the Lord, are true and righteous altogether."

With malice toward none; with charity for all; with firmness in the right, as God gives us to see the right, let us strive on to finish the work we are in; to bind up the nation's wounds; to care for him who shall have borne the battle, and for his widow, and his orphan—to do all which may achieve and cherish a just, and a lasting peace, among ourselves, and with all nations.

(Endorsement)

Original manuscript of Second Inaugural presented to Major John Hay.

April 10, 1865 A. Lincoln

Last Public Address
Washington, D.C. — April 11, 1865

We meet this evening, not in sorrow, but in gladness of heart. The evacuation of Petersburg and Richmond, and the surrender of the principal insurgent army, give hope of a righteous and speedy peace whose joyous expression can not be restrained. In the midst of this, however, He from Whom all blessings flow must not be forgotten. A call for a national thanksgiving is being prepared, and will be duly promulgated. Nor must those whose harder part gives us the cause of rejoicing, be overlooked. Their honors must not be parceled out with others. I myself, was near the front, and had the high pleasure of transmitting much of the good news to you; but no part of the honor, for plan or execution, is mine. To General Grant, his skillful officers, and brave men, all belongs. The gallant Navy stood ready, but was not in reach to take active part.

By these recent successes the re-inauguration of the national authority—reconstruction—which has had a large share of thought from the first, is pressed much more closely upon our attention. It is fraught with great difficulty. Unlike the case of a war between independent nations, there is no authorized organ for us to treat with. No one man has authority to give up the rebellion for any other man. We simply must begin with, and mould from, disorganized and discordant elements. Nor is it a small additional embarrassment that we, the loyal people, differ among ourselves as to the mode, manner, and means of reconstruction.

As a general rule, I abstain from reading the reports of attacks upon myself, wishing not to be provoked by that to which I can not properly offer an answer. In spite of this precaution, however, it comes to my knowledge that I am much censured for some supposed agency in setting up, and seeking

to sustain, the new State Government of Louisiana. In this I have done just so much as, and no more than, the public knows. In the Annual Message of December 1863 and accompanying Proclamation, I presented a plan of re-construction (as the phrase goes) which, I promised, if adopted by any State should be acceptable to, and sustained by the Executive government of the nation. I distinctly stated that this was not the only plan which might possibly be acceptable; and I also distinctly protested that the Executive claimed no right to say when, or whether members should be admitted to seats in Congress from such States.

This plan was, in advance, submitted to the then Cabinet, and distinctly approved by every member of it. One of them suggested that I should then, and in that connection, apply the Emancipation Proclamation to the theretofore excepted parts of Virginia and Louisiana; that I should drop the suggestion about apprenticeship for freed-people, and that I should omit the protest against my own power, in regard to the admission of members to Congress; but even he approved every part and parcel of the plan which has since been employed or touched by the action of Louisiana. The new constitution of Louisiana, declaring emancipation for the whole state, practically applies the Proclamation to the part previously excepted. It does not adopt apprenticeship for freed-people; and it is silent, as it could well not be otherwise, about the admission of members to Congress. So that, as it applies to Louisiana, every member of the Cabinet fully approved the plan.

The message went to Congress, and I received

many commendations of the plan, written and verbal, and not a single objection to it, from any professed emancipationist, came to my knowledge, until after the news reached Washington that the people of Louisiana had begun to move in accordance with it. From about July 1862, I had corresponded with different persons, supposed to be interested, seeking a reconstruction of a State government for Louisiana. When the Message of 1863, with the plan before mentioned, reached New Orleans, General Banks wrote me that he was confident the people, with his military co-operation, would reconstruct, substantially on that plan. I wrote him, and some of them, to try it; they tried it, and the result is known. Such only has been my agency in getting up the Louisiana government. As to sustaining it, my promise is out, as before stated. But, as bad promises are better broken than kept, I shall treat this as a bad promise, and break it, whenever I shall be convinced that keeping it is adverse to the public interest. But I have not yet been so convinced. . . .

We all agree that the seceded States, so called, are out of their proper practical relation with the Union; and that the sole object of the government, civil and military, in regard to those States is to again get them into that proper practical relation. I believe it is not only possible, but in fact, easier, to do this, without deciding, or even considering, whether these states have even been out of the Union, than with it. Finding themselves safely at home, it would be utterly immaterial whether they had ever been abroad. Let us all join in doing the acts necessary to restoring the proper practical relations between these states and the Union; and each forever after, innocently indulge his own opinion whether, in doing the acts, he brought the States from without, into the Union, or only gave them proper assistance, they never having been out of it.

The amount of constituency, so to speak, on which the new Louisiana government rests, would be more satisfactory to all, if it contained fifty, thirty, or even twenty thousand, instead of only about twelve thousand, as it does. It is also unsatisfactory to some that the elective franchise is not given to the colored man. I would myself prefer that it were now conferred on the very intelligent, and on those who serve our cause as soldiers. Still the question is not whether the Louisiana government, as it stands, is quite all that is desirable. The question is "Will it be wiser to take it as it is, and help to improve it; or to reject, and disperse it?" "Can Louisiana be brought into proper practical relation with the Union sooner by sustaining, or by discarding her new State Government?"

Some twelve thousand voters in the heretofore slave-state of Louisiana have sworn allegiance to the Union, assumed to be the rightful political power of the State, held elections, organized a State government, adopted a free-state constitution, giving the benefit of public schools equally to black and white, and empowering the Legislature to confer the elective franchise upon the colored man. Their Legislature has already voted to ratify the constitutional amendment recently passed by Congress, abolishing slavery throughout the nation. These twelve thousand persons are thus fully committed to the

Union, and to perpetual freedom in the state—committed to the very things, and nearly all the things, the nation wants—and they ask the nation's recognition, and its assistance to make good their committal. Now, if we reject and spurn them, we do our utmost to disorganize and disperse them. We in effect say to the white man "You are worthless, or worse—we will neither help you, nor be helped by you." To the blacks we say "This cup of liberty which these, your old masters, hold to your lips, we will dash from you, and leave you to the chances of gathering the spilled and scattered contents in some vague and undefined when, where, and how." If this course, discouraging and paralyzing both white and black, has any tendency to bring Louisiana into proper practical relations with the Union, I have so far, been unable to perceive it. If, on the contrary, we recognize, and sustain the new government of Louisiana, the converse of all this is made true. We encourage the hearts, and nerve the arms of the twelve thousand to adhere to their work, and argue for it, and proselyte for it, and fight for it, and feed it, and grow it, and ripen it to a complete success. The colored man too, in seeing all united for him, is inspired with vigilance, and energy, and daring, to the same end. Grant that he desires the elective franchise, will he not attain it sooner by saving the already advanced steps toward it, than by running backward over them? Concede that the new government of Louisiana is only to what it should be as the egg is to the fowl, we shall sooner have the fowl by hatching the egg than by smashing it. Again, if we reject Louisiana, we also reject one vote in favor of the proposed amendment to the national constitution. . . .

I repeat the question. Can Louisiana be brought into proper practical relation with the Union sooner by sustaining or by discarding her new State Government?

What has been said of Louisiana will apply generally to other States. And yet so great peculiarities pertain to each state; and such important and sudden changes occur in the same state; and, withal, so new and unprecedented is the whole case, that no exclusive, and inflexible plan can safely be prescribed as to details and collaterals. Such exclusive, and inflexible plan, would surely become a new entanglement. Important principles may, and must be inflexible.

In the present "situation" as the phrase goes, it may be my duty to make some new announcement to the people of the South. I am considering, and shall not fail to act, when satisfied that action will be proper.

The only house that Lincoln ever owned is at the corner of Jackson Street and Eighth Street in Springfield, Illinois. Lincoln bought it for $1,500 in 1844 from the Rev. Charles Dresser, the Episcopal rector who had married the Lincolns in 1842. Lincoln was living here when he was elected President in 1860.

Lincoln and his son Willie can be seen standing on the terrace near the corner. His youngest son Tad can barely be seen peeking from behind the corner post. The two boys standing on the sidewalk have not been identified.

The picture was taken by John Adams Whipple of Boston during the summer of 1860. The cameraman stood near the southwest corner, facing toward the northeast. *Courtesy of the Illinois State Historical Library, Old State Capitol, Springfield, Illinois.*

Chronology of Events in the Life of Lincoln

The following Chronology of Events in the Life of Lincoln contains only those names, places, dates, and events which are most important for ready reference in orienting the reader. For complete biographical information on Abraham Lincoln, the reader should consult the recommended Listing of References in the Appendix.

Pre-1809

1778. January 6. Thomas Lincoln, father of Abraham Lincoln, was born in Rockingham County, Virginia.

1782. Thomas Lincoln, with his parents, migrated to Kentucky.

1784. February 5. Nancy Hanks, mother of Abraham Lincoln, was born in western Virginia, Campbell County.

1806. June 12. Thomas Lincoln and Nancy Hanks were married in Washington County, Kentucky. Thomas Lincoln worked as a carpenter, wheelwright, and farmer.

1807. February 10. Sarah, the first child of Thomas and Nancy Lincoln, was born at Elizabethtown, Kentucky.

1808. Early in the year, Thomas Lincoln and family lived on the Bromfield Farm in Hardin County, Kentucky. Later in the year the family moved to a farm on the south fork of Nolin Creek in Hardin County, Kentucky, now Larue County, Kentucky.

1809

February 12. Abraham Lincoln, the second child of Thomas and Nancy Lincoln, was born in a log cabin at the Sinking Spring Farm on the south fork of Nolin Creek, Hardin County, Kentucky, three miles from Hodgensville, and thirteen miles from Elizabethtown, Kentucky.

1811

Spring. The Thomas Lincoln family moved to a better farm of 230 acres on Knob Creek, six miles from Hodgensville. Lincoln's first recollections were of the Knob Creek farm.

Autumn. Thomas, the third child of Thomas and Nancy Lincoln, was born, and died in infancy.

1816

Spring. At age seven, Abraham and his sister Sarah, age nine, attended A.B.C. school for two months, taught by Zachariah Riney.

Autumn. With sister Sarah, Abraham attended another A.B.C. school, four miles from the Lincoln cabin, for about three months, Caleb Hazel was the teacher.

December. The Thomas Lincoln family moved to Spencer County, Indiana, one mile east of the Crossroads that became Gentryville. With other families, the Lincoln cabin became known as the Pigeon Creek settlement.

1817

Summer. Thomas Lincoln built a log cabin as the family home to replace the "half-face" camp occupied during the winter of 1816-1817.

Autumn. Thomas and Elizabeth Sparrow (uncle and aunt of Nancy Lincoln) and their ward Dennis Hanks (age nineteen—a nephew of Mrs. Sparrow) moved to Indiana and settled in the half-face camp on the Thomas Lincoln property.

1818

September. Thomas and Elizabeth Sparrow died of the milk-sickness disease (typhoid fever). They were nursed by Nancy Lincoln.

October 5. Nancy Hanks Lincoln, mother of Abraham Lincoln, also died from the milk-sickness disease. Her coffin was built by her husband Thomas and son Abraham.

Winter of 1818-1819. Hard times for the Thomas Lincoln household, including Thomas, the widower, age forty, Sarah, age twelve, Abraham age ten, and Dennis Hanks, age twenty.

1819

Spring and summer. Young Abe was trained at home to the burdens of coarse manual farm labor.

November. Thomas Lincoln returned to Elizabethtown, Kentucky, to court Sarah Bush Johnston whose husband had died.

December 2. Thomas Lincoln married Sarah Bush Johnston. After paying off his wife's debts of about $20, Thomas Lincoln then departed from Kentucky to return to Indiana with his wife and her three children; Elizabeth Johnston, age twelve, Matilda Johnston, age eight, and John D. Johnston, age five.

1820

February. Young Abe Lincoln, his sister Sarah, and the three Johnston children, received several weeks of schooling under Andrew Crawford.

Winter and Spring. Sarah Bush Johnston Lincoln held strong influence over the Lincoln household, insisting on some schooling, when it was available, for the children, and working hard herself to improve the condition and comfort of the Lincoln cabin.

1822

Spring. Abraham, his sister Sarah, and the Johnston children attended school for one month under James Swaney.

1823

Winter. Abraham Lincoln, and the other four children in his household, attended a Blab School for several weeks under Azel Dorsey.

1824

Spring. At age fifteen, Abraham Lincoln was hired out by his father to do farm work for neighbors.

Autumn. By now, Abraham Lincoln had read every book in the Gentryville area, including: *Robinson Crusoe; Pilgrim's Progress; Aesop's Fables;* Grimshaw's *History of the United States;* Weem's *Life of Washington;* and Webster's *Elementary Spelling,* and The Holy Bible.

1825

Summer. By now Abraham Lincoln's father and step mother were active members of the Pigeon Creek Baptist Church. Thomas Lincoln had joined the church by letter of June 7, 1823. Religious discussion by adults were often overheard by young Abe.

1826

Summer. At age seventeen, Abe Lincoln hired out for thirty-seven cents per day to help James Taylor operate a ferryboat at the mouth of Anderson Creek on the Ohio River.

1827

Summer. At age eighteen, Abe Lincoln continued to do farm work for several landowners in the area. Although he was known as a good worker and excellent railsplitter, young Abe preferred to read books whenever he could find any to read.

1828

January 20. Abe Lincoln's sister Sarah, who had married Aaron Grigsby on August 2, 1826, died in childbirth in her twenty-first year of life.

Summer-Autumn. For three months, at age nineteen, Abe Lincoln hired out with Allen Gentry to take a load of farm produce by flatboat to New Orleans, returning back up the Mississippi River by steamer. Lincoln received $24 pay for the trip.

1829

Spring, Summer, Autumn. Abe Lincoln was hired out by his father to do farm work for neighboring farmers.

1830

February 20. Thomas Lincoln sold his farm in Indiana to Charles Grigsby for $125. John Hanks, who had left the Lincoln household in 1821, had written various letters about the richness of the land in Central Illinois. Those reports beckoned Thomas westward.

March 1. Thomas Lincoln's family, and the families of Mrs. Lincoln's two married daughters, a party of thirteen persons, started for Illinois. Abraham Lincoln now twenty-one years of age drove one of the three ox wagons.

March 22. The Thomas Lincoln family arrived at a spot about five miles west of Decatur, Illinois, on the north bank of the Sangamon River.

Spring. A log cabin was built by Thomas Lincoln, his son Abraham, his stepson John Johnston, and John Hanks. They cleared fifteen acres, fenced it with split rails, and planted corn.

Summer. Abraham Lincoln, now past twenty-one years old, left home and hired out to split 3,000 rails for William Warwick, the county sheriff.

1831

Winter. The extremely severe winter of 1830-1831 with record-breaking snowfall, created hardships for Thomas Lincoln and his remaining family. Thomas decided to move back to Indiana, abandoned his Sangamon River Cabin, and when weather warmed up, he headed eastward. However, he settled instead in Coles County, Illinois. The last of his homes, eight miles south of Charleston, Illinois, is now the Lincoln Log Cabin State Park.

March. Abraham Lincoln, John D. Johnston and John Hanks, paddled a canoe down the Sangamon River to New Salem, northwest of Springfield. Then Lincoln helped to build a flatboat and contracted to take a boat load of farm produce to New Orleans for Denton Offutt. (Lincoln's second trip down the Mississippi River)

April-July. Trip by flatboat to New Orleans for Denton Offutt.

Late July. Lincoln arrived back in New Salem and became a store clerk for Offutt. Gained a reputation as a story teller.

Autumn. Abe Lincoln joined the New Salem Debating Society and became known as an intellectual.

1832

March 9. Lincoln announced his candidacy as a Whig for the State Legislature.

April 7. Lincoln was elected a captain in the 31st Regiment of the Illinois Militia, and served for two months in the Black Hawk War, but saw no fighting.

July. Arrived back in New Salem shortly before election day. Carried New Salem but lost the election in the rest of the county.

1833

January. Lincoln and William F. Berry purchased the New Salem store formerly owned by Reuben Radford, but they kept going deeper into debt. Finally the store "winked out." More than ten years passed before Lincoln fully paid off his debts from this enterprise.

May 7. Lincoln was appointed Postmaster of New Salem, Illinois. He conducted his duties at his store until the post office was moved to Petersburg in 1836.

1834

January. As a deputy surveyor for Sangamon County, Lincoln's first survey was of 800 acres for Reason Shipley.

Spring. Lincoln announced his candidacy for the State Legislature. He made a few speeches, campaigned quietly from his post office and on surveying trips, received bipartisan support and was elected on August 4. He was reelected in 1836, 1838, and 1840.

Summer. By purchasing Blackstone's *Commentaries on the Laws of England* and Chittys *Pleadings*, Lincoln began his study of law.

November. In order to buy suitable clothes as a legislator, Lincoln borrowed $200. He rode the stagecoach to Vandalia, the Illinois State Capital.

Winter. 1834-35. At Vandalia, Lincoln's roommate was John T. Stuart, also from Sangamon County. Stuart encouraged Lincoln to study law. Lincoln's salary for the session was $258 with which he repaid the loan.

1835

Spring. Back at New Salem, Lincoln continued to be postmaster, ran his store, served as clerk at elections, split rails, and surveyed land in the area.

Summer. Ann Rutledge died. She was a beautiful girl of twenty-two with whom Lincoln had formed a strong friendship.

December 7. Lincoln attended the special session of the State Legislature where he successfully promoted his own pet project—the Beardstown and Sangamon Canal.

1836

March 24. Lincoln was certified by the Sangamon Circuit Court as a person of good moral character who should be permitted to take the state bar examination. Then he announced he would run for reelection to the State Legislature.

Summer. Lincoln campaigned thoroughly, was reelected, and led the entire Whig ticket. He surveyed the townsites for Petersburg, Huron, Albany, and Bath.

September 9. Lincoln passed the Illinois State Bar Examination administered by the Illinois Supreme Court, and received a license to practice law.

Autumn. Lincoln began a courtship of Mary Owens who eventually turned down his offer of marriage.

December 5. At the beginning of the Tenth General Assembly at Vandalia, Lincoln was selected as Whig floor leader.

1837

January-February. As leader of the "Long Nine" (all nine were over six feet tall) from Sangamon County, Lincoln guided the famous $10,000,000 Internal Improvements Bills through the Assembly.

February. Lincoln successfully led the movement to relocate the state capital to Springfield.

March 3. With Dan stone, Lincoln entered their protest in the *House journal* against the anti-abolitionist resolutions which the House had passed on January 20. Lincoln did not argue the constitutionality of slavery, but he did attack the moral injustice of slavery.

April 15. Lincoln left new Salem, moved to Springfield and took lodging above a store kept by Joshua F. speed who became his closest friend. On the same day he became the law partner of John T. Stuart.

July 10-22. Lincoln attended the special session of the Illinois Tenth General Assembly at Vandalia.

1838

January 27. Lincoln spoke before the young Men's Lyceum of Springfield, stressing the dangers of mobs and the need for law and order.

Summer. Lincoln ran for his third term for the state Legislature, did little campaigning, and was elected by a large margin.

July. Lincoln attended the special session of the state Legislature to deal with the panic of 1838. He became concerned over mob actions at the murder of Elijah P. Lovejoy at Alton and other murders relating to slavery and abolition.

December. Attending the Eleventh General Assembly at Vandalia before the capital moved to Springfield, Lincoln was again chosen Whig floor leader, but he was defeated for speaker of the House.

1839

January-February. In the General assembly, Lincoln supported a tax of 25 cents per $100 of assessed valuation on all property in Illinois.

Spring. Lincoln joined the political movement to nominate William Henry Harrison for president in 1840.

June 24. Lincoln was elected a trustee of Springfield town.

July 4. Illinois state government was officially moved from Vandalia to Springfield.

September 23. Lincoln began to practice law on the newly organized Eighth Judical Circuit, and continued to "ride this circuit" until nominated for the presidency.

October 8. Lincoln was chosen a presidential elector by the Whig Convention, and was likewise chosen for the elections of 1844, 1852, and 1856.

December 3. Lincoln was admitted to practice in the United States Circuit Court.

December 16. Lincoln, age thirty, met Mary Todd, age twenty-one, from Lexington, Kentucky, who came to reside in Springfield with her sister Mrs. Ninian W. Edwards. Thereafter, Lincoln took an active interest in all social and cultural meetings in Springfield.

1840

Summer. Lincoln was elected to his fourth term in the State legislature.

November 23-December 5. Lincoln attended the first session of the Twelfth general Assembly, the House meeting in the Methodist Church.

December 7. Lincoln attended the second session of the Twelfth General Assembly, both the House and the Senate meeting in the new Capitol building. The session adjourned March 1, 1841. Lincoln became engaged to Mary Todd and later broke off the engagement.

1841

January. Illness during the last part of December 1840 and early January caused Lincoln to miss legislative sessions for about three weeks. He suffered deep melancholy, and wrote letters admitting his "discreditable hypochondriaism."

April 14. Lincoln's law partnership with Stuart was dissolved, and a new partnership was formed with Stephen T. Logan.

August. Lincoln visited the home of his close friend Joshua F. Speed who had moved to Farmington, near Louisville, Kentucky. He stayed for three weeks, giving comfort and advice to Speed who was brooding over whether or not to get married. Lincoln advised him to do so.

September. Lincoln returned with Speed to Springfield. Then he worked harder than ever at his law practice. Speed returned to Louisville in December.

1842

Spring. Lincoln received letters from Speed, who had married, saying that his melancholy had completely disappeared, and that Lincoln himself should marry.

November 4. Abraham Lincoln and Mary Todd were married by the Rev. Charles Dresser, Episcopalian minister.

Autumn-Winter. Lincoln's law practice grew larger. His yearly income of $1,500 compared favorably with the salaries of the Governor—$1,200, and the circuit judges—$750.

1843

Spring-Summer. Lincoln's study and practice of law became extremely academic and painstaking under the guidance of his new partner Logan who gave Lincoln only one-third of all fees collected. Their firm, Logan and Lincoln, became one of the best in Illinois.

August 1. Robert Todd Lincoln, the first child of the Lincolns was born at the Globe Tavern.

Summer. Lincoln was interested in running for Congress, But agreed to "take his turn" after John J. Hardin of Jacksonville and Edward Baker of Springfield.

Autumn. Lincoln was proposed as the Whig candidate for Governor of Illinois, but he refused to encourage the idea.

1844

January 16. Lincoln purchased the Rev. Charles Dresser home at 8th and Jackson Street for $1,500.

Summer. Lincoln stumped the state speaking for Henry Clay for president. In the national election, James K. Polk carried Illinois and the nation, and was elected.

December 2. Lincoln's law partnership with Logan ended when Logan expressed a desire to take his own son into the firm.

December 9. Lincoln's next, and last, law office was set up with newly licensed William H. Herndon as his junior partner. Herndon's scholarly and technical use of the law often deferred to Lincoln's methodical analysis which Herndon labeled as "pitiless and persistent in pursuit of truth."

1845

Spring. Lincoln supported Edward D. Baker as the Whig candidate to Congress. Baker was elected.

November. Baker assured Lincoln that he would not run for reelection and would support Lincoln. However, Hardin decided to run again.

Winter, 1845-46. Sparring between Hardin and Lincoln over Whig support for Congress resulted in Hardin discrediting himself. Hardin then withdrew.

1846

March 10. Edward Baker Lincoln, the second son of the Lincolns, was named after Congressman Edward D. Baker.

May 1. Lincoln was nominated for the U.S. Congress by the Whig District Convention meeting in Petersburg.

May 30. Lincoln supported the Declaration of War against Mexico aiming to expel the Mexicans from land between the Nueces and Rio Grande rivers.

Summer. Lincoln campaigned successfully for Congress. Voting scored 6,340 for Lincoln and 4,829 for Cartwright. He became the only Whig among the seven Congressmen from Illinois.

1847

July. Lincoln made his first trip to Chicago to attend a state internal improvements convention where he met Horace Greeley, Daniel Webster, Edward Bates and other national leaders.

Autumn. Lincoln represented Robert Matson, a slaveowner, at the Coles County Court House in Charleston. Matson tried to regain possession of a slave family that escaped and claimed freedom because they were brought by their owner, Matson, into the free state of Illinois. Lincoln showed little enthusiasm for his client and lost the case.

Autumn. Before leaving Springfield for Congress, Lincoln gave no support to the national war fever for conquering all of Mexico. He believed that the U.S. had surpassed its war objectives.

October 25. With his family, Lincoln left Springfield for Washington, D.C., visiting en route at Lexington, Kentucky, with relatives of Mrs. Lincoln.

December 6. Lincoln began his term as a Whig Congressman from Illinois. Other House members included: former President John Quincy Adams, George Ashmun, Alexander H. Stephens, Caleb B. Smith, and Andrew Johnson. Senators included Henry Clay, Daniel Webster, John C. Calhoun, Hannibal Hamlin, Jefferson Davis, and Stephen A. Douglas.

December 22. Lincoln introduced in the House his Eight Spot Resolutions intending to force President Polk to admit that Mexico, and not the United States, held jurisdiction over the spot where the war started.

1848

January 12. Lincoln addressed the House with a strong denunciation of President Polk for continuing the war against helpless Mexico.

January-February. Back in Illinois, where war fever had reached a high pitch, Lincoln was condemned by many Democrats and Whigs as a friend of the enemy.

June 7-9. Lincoln attended the Whig National Convention in Philadelphia and helped to nominate General Zachary Taylor for President.

August-September. Lincoln campaigned for Taylor in Maryland, Massachussetts, and New York.

Autumn. Lincoln campaigned in Illinois for Taylor who carried the state and the nation.

December. Lincoln returned to Washington, D.C. for the second session of the Thirtieth Congress. He did not run for reelection. He worked hard for all Whig causes, and he supported all efforts to exclude slavery from newly acquired territory from Mexico.

1849

January 10. Lincoln read in Congress the draft of a bill for compensated abolition of slavery in the District of Columbia. Finding that his supporters deserted him, he never formally introduced the bill.

March 7. Lincoln was admitted to practice law in the U.S. Supreme Court. His only case there he lost.

March. After Congress adjourned, Lincoln stayed on in Washington to work on patronage problems, but found that his influence was small.

May 22. Lincoln received a patent for combining adjustable buoyant chambers on steam boats in shallow water.

June 21. Lincoln failed to get the appointment as commissioner of the General Land Office.

Summer. When the Sangamon Circuit Court convened, Lincoln returned to practicing law in Illinois.

August 21. Lincoln declined the presidential appointment as secretary of Oregon Territory.

September 27. Lincoln declined the presidential appointment as governor of Oregon.

1850

February 1. Edward Baker Lincoln, age four, second son of the Lincoln's, died of consumption.

Spring-Summer-Autumn. Lincoln took no part in Illinois politics leading up to the Compromise of 1850. Occasionally he suffered gloom over his failure during his one term in Congress.

December 21. William Wallace Lincoln, the third son of the Lincolns, was born.

1851

January 15. Abraham Lincoln's father, Thomas Lincoln, died in Coles County, Illinois.

Spring, Summer, Autumn. Lincoln grew steadily in skill and stature as an honest lawyer. He handled increasingly more important cases; and he read extensively from the law, the Bible, and the plays of Shakespeare.

1852

July 6. At a public memorial ceremony in the Illinois House of Representatives, Springfield, Lincoln delivered a eulogy on Henry Clay, his ideal as a statesman, who had died on June 29, 1852.

Summer, Autumn. Lincoln campaigned for General Winfield Scott, Whig candidate for president.

1853

April 4. Thomas Lincoln (known as Tad), the fourth son of the Lincolns, was born.

Autumn. Nebraska's petition for organization as a territory drew little notice from Lincoln. The first bill reported out of committee in Congress made no reference to slavery.

1854

January 23. Senator Stephen A. Douglas, whose Committee on Territories reported out a new bill allowing for two territories with popular sovereignty on the slavery issue, predicted; "It will raise a hell of a storm." In Illinois, Lincoln became academically opposed to repeal of the Missouri Compromise as provided in the new bill by Douglas.

March 4. The Kansas-Nebraska Bill, with repeal of the Missouri Compromise, passed the Senate.

May 30. The Kansas-Nebraska Bill, with repeal of the Missouri Compromise, passed the House, and was signed into law. As Lincoln later wrote: "I was losing interest in politics, when the repeal of the Missouri Compromise aroused me again."

Spring, Summer. Lincoln did not attend the newly-organizing groups called Anti-Nebraska Men and Republicans.

August. Lincoln reentered politics to campaign for the reelection of Whig Congressman Richard Yates, but he immediately drew attention to himself as a potential leader of antislavery forces.

October 3. Lincoln attended the speech by Senator Douglas defending popular sovereignty at the Illinois State Fair. Pressured by his friends, Lincoln agreed to answer Douglas on the following day.

October 4. At the Illinois State Capitol, Lincoln delivered an answer in depth to Douglas. Immediately he was recognized as the leader of all opposition to Douglas.

October 16. At Peoria, Lincoln repeated his speech, of three hours length, given at Springfield on October 4. He emphasized that he had no prejudice against the Southern people and their constitutional right to own slaves. He stressed that he only opposed the extension of slavery.

November 7. Lincoln was elected to the Illinois House of Representatives, but he resigned his seat before taking it in order to be the Whig Candidate for the U.S. Senate.

1855

February 8. The election by the Illinois Legislature of U.S. Senator involved a three-way split of votes for Lincoln (Whig) 44, Shields (Democrat) 41, and Trumbull (Anti-Nebraska Democrat) 5. Subsequently, Lincoln gave his support to Trumbull in order to prevent the election of a proslavery candidate, Joel Matteson.

March. Lincoln gave careful attention to the troubles in Kansas regarding homesteading by proslavery men and antislavery men.

1855 to 1860. Period of success for Lincoln as a lawyer who handled many important law suits involving railroads, river steamboat traffic, banks, insurance companies, and large manufacturing corporations. Also, he often handled cases for friends, refusing a fee.

1856

February 22. Lincoln attended a convention of Anti-Nebraska editors at Decatur, Illinois.

May 29. Lincoln delivered his famous Lost Speech at a Republican Party Convention in Bloomington, Illinois. That speech gave new birth to the Illinois Republican Party which thereafter absorbed most of the Anti-Nebraska Democrats, Whigs, Free-Soilers, and Know-Nothings. Lincoln was made a presidential elector and later gave many campaign speeches for Fremont for president.

June. The National Democratic Party Convention in Cincinnati, Ohio, nominated James Buchanan for president, and John Breckenridge of Kentucky for vice-president.

June 17. The National Republican Party Convention in Philadelphia nominated John C. Fremont of California for president, and William Dayton of New Jersey for vice-president. Abraham Lincoln of Illinois received 110 votes for vice-president but was not present at the convention and was not nationally known.

Late June. A minority of diehard Whigs split from the Republican Convention and nominated ex-President Millard Fillmore for president and Andrew Donelson for vice-president.

Summer. Many Southern leaders threatened secession if Fremont were elected.

Autumn. Buchanan was elected. Electoral College votes were: Buchanan 174, Fremont 114, and Fillmore 8. Buchanan carried Illinois but all state offices went Republican. Buchanan's popular vote was considerably less, nationally, than the combined vote for Fremont and Fillmore.

1857

March 4. Inauguration of James Buchanan as president saw relative calm in the country. "Bleeding Kansas" had been quieted by U.S. Troops.

March 6. The U.S. Supreme Court announced (five to four vote) that a negro, Dred Scott, had no right to sue in a Federal Court, that territories could not prohibit slavery, and that Congress could not prohibit slavery from a territory.

Spring. In righteous wrath, Republicans all over the country protested the Dred Scott decision. In the New England States, public meetings even clamored for secession. Lincoln disagreed with the Supreme Court ruling, but he gave no support to disunion. Douglas announced that his policy of popular sovereignty was not dead, and did not prevent the people of a territory from excluding slavery. Douglas reasoned that by a territorial legislature refusing to give slavery local protection, the people could effectually exclude slavery.

June 26. In the evening at the state capitol in Springfield, Lincoln replied in depth (three hours) to the position of Douglas on the Dred Scott decision. Lincoln declared that the decision must be obeyed, even though it was erroneous. He refuted Douglas's "counterfeit logic" that Republican opposition to the Dred Scott decision endorsed complete racial equality, including marriage between the races.

August 12. Lincoln received a fee of $5,000 (his largest fee for a single case) for winning a case for the Illinois Central Railroad.

Autumn. A split between Senator Douglas and President Buchanan, over the Lecompton Constitution for Kansas, brought many Eastern Republicans into support for the reelection of Douglas to the Senate. But in Illinois, Republicans began to campaign for Lincoln for the Senate in 1858.

1858

April 6. Lincoln delivered a lecture on Discoveries and Inventions in Bloomington, Illinois. This same lecture with slight variations was given later about six times at other cities in the Mid-West.

May 7. At Beardstown, Illinois, Lincoln cleared Duff Armstrong of the charge of murder. On hearing that the son of his old New Salem friend Jack Armstrong was unable to pay a lawyer, Lincoln dropped all other business and offered to defend Duff. By using an almanac, Lincoln discredited the state's star witness who claimed to have seen by moonlight Duff Armstrong strike the man who died. Lincoln refused any fee for his services in the case.

June 16. The Illinois State Republican Convention nominated Abraham Lincoln as "the first and only choice of Republicans of Illinois for the United States Senate" as the successor to Stephen A. Douglas.

July 9. The U.S. Senatorial contest in Illinois began in Chicago from the balcony of the Tremont House (Hotel) with Douglas addressing an enthusiastic audience.

July 10. Also at the Tremont House in Chicago, Lincoln answered the Douglas speech. Public support for Lincoln's arguments began to grow.

July 17. Douglas addressed a large crowd at Springfield in the afternoon. Lincoln spoke to an equally large audience in the evening. Several days later, Lincoln challenged Douglas to a series of joint debates. Douglas agreed, on certain conditions. Lincoln accepted the conditions.

August 21. At Ottawa, the first of the Lincoln-Douglas debates, Douglas spoke first.

August 27. At Freeport, the second of the Lincoln-Douglas debates, Lincoln spoke first.

September 15. At Jonesboro, the third of the Lincoln-Douglas debates, Douglas spoke first.

September 18. At Charleston, the fourth of the Lincoln-Douglas debates, Lincoln spoke first.

October 7. At Galesburg, the fifth of the Lincoln-Douglas debates, Douglas spoke first.

October 13. At Quincy, the sixth of the Lincoln-Douglas debates, Lincoln spoke first.

October 15. At Alton, the seventh of the Lincoln-Douglas debates, Douglas spoke first.

November 2. Election results gave more popular votes to Lincoln than to Douglas, but the outdated legislative districts elected more Democrats than Republicans to the State Legislature, thus assuring the reelection, by the legislature, of Douglas.

November, December. Lincoln wrote various letters to friends urging them to stand firm on the issues of the campaign just ended, but pledging himself not to run against Trumbull for the Senate in 1860.

1859

Winter, Spring. Lincoln was mentioned frequently in all parts of the country as a worthwhile presidential candidate for 1860, by reason of his clear thinking on the issues of his debates with Douglas. Lincoln gave no outward support to the idea, but he began to accept invitations to speak at public events all across the nation.

August. Lincoln gave public addresses at Council Bluffs, Iowa, and at St. Joseph, Missouri.

September. Lincoln gave public addresses at Columbus, Dayton, Hamilton and Cincinnati in Ohio, and at Indianapolis, Indiana. On most of these occasions he refuted the policies of Douglas.

September 30. Lincoln addressed the Wisconsin State Agricultural Society at Milwaukee during the Wisconsin State Fair, regarding agriculture and labor.

October 1-2. Lincoln gave speeches at Beloit and Janesville, Wisconsin.

October. John Brown's attack on the federal arsenal at Harper's Ferry was overcome by Colonel Robert E. Lee with Virginia militiamen and U.S. Marines. Lincoln admired John Brown's philosophy and courage, but he labeled his lawlessness as indefensible.

November 20-December 3. Lincoln made a speaking tour in Kansas at Elwood, Troy, Doniphan, Atchison, and Leavenworth.

December. Lincoln began to listen to demands that he become an avowed candidate for president in the 1860 elections.

December 20. Lincoln sent a requested autobiographical sketch to Jesse Fell who distributed it to various Eastern newspapers to promote Lincoln as a presidential candidate who took a moderate stand on slavery.

Late December. Norman Judd, Illinois Republican state chairman, and Lincoln's campaign manager in 1858, visited the Republican National Committee in New York to invite the national convention to meet in Chicago in 1860. The invitation was accepted.

1860

February 16. The *Chicago Tribune* came out for Lincoln for president.

February 27. Lincoln delivered a speech at the Cooper Union Institute in New York City. In this famous address, Lincoln painstakingly refuted the claim by Douglas that our founding fathers intended to forbid the federal government from controlling slavery in the territories.

Early March. Following his highly successful speech at New York City, Lincoln began a two-week speaking tour of towns in New England, including Providence, Concord, Dover, Manchester, and Hartford. At Exeter, New Hampshire, Lincoln spoke, and visited with his son Robert who was attending Phillips Exeter Academy.

April 23. The Democratic National Convention, meeting in Charleston, South Carolina, broke down over the moral issue of slavery. The Southern states were disenchanted with Douglas who, during the Lincoln-Douglas debates, had explained how a Northern territory could keep slavery out of a territory by not passing local "protective legislation." Douglas had expected Southern gratitude for his designing the Kansas-Nebraska Bill to explicitly repeal the Compromise of 1820.

Douglas's forces succeeded in recessing the Convention to June 18 to meet in Baltimore (after the Republican Convention had met). The Alabama faction recessed their half of the convention to meet on June 11, in Richmond, Virginia.

May 9-10. Lincoln attended the Illinois State Republican Convention at Decatur. The Convention unanimously instructed the state delegation to the National Convention in Chicago to vote for Lincoln, "the Railsplitter" for president.

May 16. The Republican National Convention opened at The Wigwam in Chicago. Two days were spent in adopting a party platform, and in lining up votes for Seward of New York, Chase of Ohio, Bates of Missouri, Cameron of Pennsylvania, Dayton of New Jersey, and Lincoln of Illinois.

May 18. On the third ballot, Abraham Lincoln was nominated for the presidency of the United States. Hannibal Hamlin of Maine was nominated for vice-president.

June 11. The Alabama Faction from the Democratic Convention at Charleston met first informally in Baltimore to nominate Breckinridge of Kentucky for president, and then met officially in Richmond to endorse Breckinridge and a platform of positive protection of slavery.

June 18. The Northern Democrats meeting in Baltimore as the reconvened Charleston Convention, nominated Stephen A. Douglas for president.

June 25. The Constitutional Union Party also met at Baltimore to nominate John Bell of Tennessee for president and Edward Everett of Massachussetts for vice-president.

Summer. With his opposition split three ways among supporters of Douglas, Breckinridge, and Bell, Lincoln conducted no elaborated campaign. He showed only moderate alarm over threats of Southern secession if the Republicans won. Douglas campaigned strenuously.

Autumn. State elections in Ohio and Pennsylvania showed a strong Republican trend. Aware that Mr. Lincoln would certainly be elected president, Douglas forsook his own campaign and went South to try to save the Union. His speechmaking was sincere and fierce for Union solidarity with no secession by any state. But the South considered him antislavery.

November 6. Election day showed popular votes of: 1,866,452 for Lincoln; 1,376,957 for Douglas; 849,781 for Breckinridge; and 588,879 for Bell. The Electoral College vote would show 173 for Lincoln, 72 for Breckinridge, 29 for Bell, and 12 for Douglas.

December. Fear gripped the South. Lincoln himself was not feared as a bad man. Only the realization that slavery as an institution was weakening, and would die, caused alarm.

December 20. South Carolina, in a state constitutional convention, seceded from the Union. Before Lincoln was inaugurated as president, the states of Mississippi, Florida, Alabama, Georgia, Louisiana, and Texas, also seceded from the Union.

1861

January. Lincoln's basic positions were reaffirmed by Senator Trumbull and others as; no interference with slavery as an institution in Southern states; enforcement of fugitive slave laws; and no extension of slavery into federal territories.

January 31. Lincoln visited Charleston and Coles County in Illinois to see his aged stepmother and old friends of the area.

February, March. Southern states remaining in the Union prior to inauguration day were; North Carolina, Tennessee, Arkansas, and Virginia. Border states staying in the Union were Maryland, Delaware, Kentucky, and Missouri.

February 4. In Montgomery, Alabama, the Confederate States of America were formed by representatives from South Carolina, Georgia, Florida, Alabama, Mississippi, and Louisiana. Texas was not represented. Jefferson Davis was elected president, and Alexander H. Stephens was elected vice-president.

February. Selections for the Lincoln cabinet included:

Sec. of State............ William Seward of New York
Sec. of Treasury ....Salmon P. Chase of Ohio
Attorney General ....Edward Bates of Missouri
Sec. of War.........Simon Cameron of Pennsylvania
Sec. of Navy...........Gideon Welles of Connecticut
Sec. of Interior..............Caleb B. Smith of Indiana
Postmaster General.Montgomery Blair of Maryland

February 11. The Lincoln family departed on a special train for Washington, D.C. In the early cold and rainy morning at the Great Western Railroad Station in Springfield, Lincoln delivered his Farewell Address.

February 11-23. At dozens of towns and cities en route to Washington, D.C., Lincoln spoke to the anxious crowds—appealing for the preservation of the Union.

February 18. Jefferson Davis at the Alabama State House became president of the Confederacy.

February 23-March 4. President-elect Lincoln and his family roomed at Willard's Hotel in Washington.

March 4. Abraham Lincoln was inaugurated as the sixteenth President of the United States. His Inaugural Address stressed;

1. The new administration would not interfere with the institution of slavery in states where it existed.

2. No state can lawfully leave the Union on its own motion.

3. No resort to force or bloodshed would be made in holding, occupying, and possessing federal property.

4. The Administration was duty bound to preserve, protect, and defend the Union.

5. The North and South were not enemies but friends whose bonds of affection must not be broken.

March 5. Word was received from Major Robert Anderson at Fort Sumter in Charleston Harbor, South Carolina, that provisions were low and if not supplied within six weeks he would be forced to abandon the fort.

March 9. Lincoln held his first cabinet meeting.

April 8. Lincoln notified Governor Pickens of South Carolina that he was sending immediately only provisions, and no guns or munitions or men, to Fort Sumter.

April 11. General Beauregard, Confederate commander at Charleston, demanded that Major Anderson surrender. Anderson answered that he would evacuate on April 15, unless he received needed provisions for staying on.

April 12. At 4:30 a.m. Confederate forces fired on Fort Sumter. Union forces fired back. Relief ships for the fort arrived, but stood their distance. The fort held out for two days before being destroyed.

April 14. Anderson surrendered. Beauregard allowed Anderson and his ninety Union soldiers to board a relief ship for New York. The Civil War had begun.

April 15. Lincoln issued a proclamation calling for 75,000 militia for three months to help defend the Union. Senator Douglas approved 'all of Lincoln's actions and pledged full support. A special session of Congress was called for July 4.

April 17. The Virginia State Convention passed an ordinance of secession, followed soon afterwards by similar actions in North Carolina, Tennessee, and Arkansas. The capital of the Confederacy was then moved to Richmond, Virginia. The border states of Delaware, Maryland, Kentucky, and Missouri stayed in the Union but supplied troops to both North and South.

April 18-30. Mobilization of Southern troops occurred more rapidly than mobilization of Union forces. More than 15,000 Confederate troops near Alexandria were ready to march on undefended Washington.

April 25. The New York Seventh Regiment arrived to help defend the capital.

May 23. Federal troops crossed the Potomac River to establish a bridgehead of forts to protect Washington. Confederate troops withdrew southward from Alexandria.

June 3. Stephen A. Douglas died in Chicago at the age of forty-eight.

June 29. A Cabinet meeting with military advisers decided in favor of a Union Army advance on Manassas Junction, a few miles south of the Potomac River bridgehead.

July 4. At the Special Session of Congress, Lincoln gave a full account of administrative philosophy of defending the Union and pursuing the war.

July 21. General Irvin McDowell, the Union commander, with 30,000 poorly trained men attacked General Beauregard at Bull Run near Manassas Junction. What seemed like a Union victory turned into a serious Union rout. Union troops retreated back into Washington which was defended by General Winfield Scott. Confederate troops did not pursue the Union Army.

July 22. General George B. McClellan was given command of the Army of the Potomac. Lincoln announced a policy of holding present positions, tightening the blockade of the South, and pushing expeditions into Virginia and Tennessee and down the Mississippi River.

July 27. The Union Army reestablished itself at Arlington Heights in Virginia across from Washington.

August 30. General John C. Fremont in Missouri took over administrative powers in the state, invoked martial law, and emancipated all slaves of Missouri citizens who took up arms against the Union. Subsequently, Lincoln requested Fremont to modify his commands to fit his military powers only. Fremont refused.

Early Autumn. General McClellan built strong defenses around Washington, but delayed any campaign into Virginia to crush the rebellion.

Autumn. Foreign relations grew serious with Great Britain. The Union warship *San Jacinto* stopped the British steamer *Trent* on the high seas and removed James Mason and John Sidell as Confederate agents to foreign nations. Eventually the prisoners were surrendered back to Britain, thus avoiding war.

October. Senators Wade, Trumbull, Chandler, and other antislavery leaders demanded a Union attack against the Confederacy. Public patience was ending.

October 21. The Battle of Ball's Bluff on the south bank of the Potomac River was a total disaster for Union forces. Although it was only a small engagement, about 1,700 men on each side, it had fearful effect on Union morale. Lincoln's personal friend, a U.S. senator from Oregon, Colonel Edward D. Baker, was killed in the battle.

October 24. General Fremont's refusal to conform his policies in Missouri to congressional and administration policies forced Lincoln to relieve him of his command.

November 1. General Winfield Scott, general-in-chief of all armies, resigned due to illness and old age. Lincoln replaced him with General McClellan who had escaped blame for the defeat at Ball's Bluff.

December 10. Congress appointed a Joint Committee of the House and Senate to investigate the conduct of the war.

1862

Early January. Congressional investigation revealed gigantic waste, corruption, and favoritism in Army administration under Secretary of War Simon Cameron. While growing in size to 500,000 men, the Army was administratively corrupt and ineffectual.

January 12. Lincoln appointed Cameron as minister to Russia. As the new secretary of war, Lincoln appointed Edwin M. Stanton who previously had ridiculed Lincoln's "painful imbecility" but who was a scrupulous wizard of organizational efficiency.

January 27. McClellan continued to delay any military campaign into Virginia. Lincoln issued General War Order Number One which instructed all armies to advance on Confederate positions on or before February 22.

February 6. General Ulysses S. Grant, captured Fort Henry, Tennessee, on the Tennessee River. This was the first important Union victory.

February 13. General Grant captured Fort Donelson, Tennessee, on the Cumberland River, taking 14,000 prisoners. In this battle he earned the name of "Unconditional Surrender Grant."

February 20. William Wallace Lincoln, age twelve, died at the White House from typhoid fever.

March 8. The Battle of Pea Ridge, Arkansas, was a Union victory by General Samuel R. Curtis.

March 9. The Confederate ironclad warship *Merrimac*, after ramming the Federal ships *Congress, Cumberland,* and *Minnesota,* was met by the Union ironclad warship *Monitor.* The Confederate ship then retreated back to Norfolk. Thereafter, wooden warships would be defenseless against ironclads.

March 10. Lincoln's plan of "compensated emancipation" of slaves passed both houses of Congress, but not one vote came from the border states. The plan, while endorsed as a policy, was never implemented with appropriations.

March 11. Lincoln removed McClellan as general-in-chief of armies and temporarily took the position for himself, but kept McClellan in command of the Army of the Potomac.

March 17. McClellan began embarking a force of 100,000 troops for sailing down the Potomac River and Chesapeake Bay to the peninsula between the York and James Rivers for a drive on Richmond. Lincoln had favored a frontal attack on Richmond through Manassas Junction, but was overruled by leading military commanders and the cabinet.

April 6. The Battle of Shiloh (Pittsburg Landing) Tennessee began with a Confederate attack on Union forces. Union armies under Grant and Sherman finally repulsed the attack, but losses on both sides were extremely high.

April 7. Union General John Pope, with the aid of gunboats, captured Island No. 10 in the Mississippi River.

April 11. Fort Pulaski, Georgia, near the entrance to Savannah, fell to Union forces.

April 12. General David Hunter, commander of the department of South, ordered all slaves around Fort Pulaski, Georgia, confiscated and emancipated. Lincoln later rescinded the order as not being within the authority of military commanders.

April 16. Lincoln signed an act of Congress freeing the slaves in the District of Columbia.

April 18. Commodore David Farragut and Commodore David Porter with Federal warships began pounding Confederate forts below New Orleans.

April 25. New Orleans, Louisiana, was captured by Union troops under General Butler. Thenceforth the largest city in the South became a base of operations against the Confederacy.

May 4. Confederate defenders evacuated Yorktown, Virginia.

May 6. Union forces occupied Williamsburg, Virginia, following a fierce battle. President Lincoln, with Secretary of War Stanton and Secretary of the Treasury Chase, arrived at Fortress Monroe, Virginia, Union base of operations.

May 7. Lincoln visited the Union warship *Monitor,* and personally planned the strategy to destroy the *Merrimac* and capture Norfolk.

May 8. Federal warships, including the *Monitor,* attacked Sewel's Point. The *Merrimac* came out from Norfolk and then retreated.

May 10. Federal troops captured Norfolk, Virginia, while President Lincoln watched. Surrendering Confederate troops numbered 6,000. The *Merrimac* was blown up by retreating defenders.

Mid-May. General McClellan made slow progress

up the peninsula, but Confederate General Stonewall Jackson was winning numerous engagements in the Shenandoah Valley.

May 15. Lincoln approved the act of Congress establishing the Department of Agriculture.

May 20. Lincoln signed the Homestead Act which granted 160 acres of public land to each settler who would occupy and improve it for five years.

May 31. The Battle of Fair Oaks (or Seven Pines) began. Confederate General Joseph Johnson, wounded, was replaced by General Robert E. Lee. General "Stonewall" Jackson, from the Shenandoah Valley, arrived with help for Lee. Both sides suffered great losses. The Union armies were not defeated, but were weakened for further attacks on Richmond.

June. Battles in Virginia around Richmond at Port Republic, Mechanicsville, Gaine's Mill, Cold Harbor, Savage's Station, and Frayser's Farm weakened both sides. McClellan wired Lincoln for 50,000 more troops.

July. The Battle of Malvern Hill, Virginia, with tremendous losses to both sides, was the last major battle of the Peninsular Campaign.

July. Lincoln signed an act for the charter for the Union Pacific Railroad Company.

July 1. Lincoln signed the Federal Income Tax Law which levied a 3 percent tax on personal incomes.

July 2. Lincoln signed the Morrill Land Grant Act which provided endowment for state agricultural schools and colleges.

July 8. Lincoln visited Fortress Monroe and Harri-son's Landing, Virginia, to inspect the army and confer with McClellan.

July 11. Lincoln appointed General Henry W. Halleck as general-in-chief of all Union armies. Halleck had been area commander of the successful campaigns of General Grant in the West.

Mid-July. A midsummer lull developed. General John Pope was placed in command of Union forces in Northern Virginia. Lee revised Confederate strategy and planned to draw Union strength away from Richmond.

July 17. Lincoln signed the Second Confiscation Act providing: that slaves of all Confederates. who supported the rebellion would be free when they came under Union control; and that the President could employ negroes for military and naval service in suppressing the rebellion.

July 22. Lincoln presented the first draft of his Emancipation Proclamation to his cabinet, and agreed to wait until after a major Union victory to announce it.

July 29. The Confederate Cruiser *Alabama* left Liverpool, England, unarmed but to be armed later to begin attacking Union shipping on the high seas.

July 30. General Halleck ordered McClellan to remove his sick and wounded back to Washington. McClellan, sensing a shift in Union strategy, requested 100,000 additional troops to attack Richmond.

August 4. Lincoln ordered a federal states draft of 300,000 militia to serve for nine months.

August 5. The Battle of Baton Rouge, Louisiana,

resulted in defeat for Confederate General John Breckinridge.

August 7. McClellan delayed responding to Halleck's order of July 30. Halleck then demanded that all of McClellan's troops should be moved northward to Aquia Creek, near Bull Run, to help General Pope who was coming under attack from General Jackson. McClellan continued to delay.

Mid-August. Knowing that McClellan's huge army was remaining static and would not attack Richmond, Generals Lee, Jackson, and Longstreet combined forces against General Pope in northern Virginia.

August 19. Horace Greeley, editor of the *New York Tribune*, condemned Lincoln's policy of not using his wartime power to emancipate all slaves.

August 22. President Lincoln responded to Greeley by writing publicly: "My paramount object in this struggle is to save the Union, and is not either to save or to destroy slavery."

August 26-30. Confederate generals converged on General Pope's Army of Northern Virginia at Manassas Junction, headquarters for the Union army, food, supplies, and munitions. The Second Battle of Bull Run was a defeat for General Pope. McClellan's relief forces had not arrived in time.

August 31. The wounded from General Pope's defeated army poured into Washington. Gloom swept the national capital.

September 1. Lincoln, McClellan, and Halleck conferred and realized that subordinate officers had no respect for General Pope.

September 2. Lincoln removed Pope of his command and placed McClellan in full command of all armies in Virginia and around Washington.

September 4. Knowing better than to attack heavily fortified Washington, General Lee and his Confederate forces moved northward into Maryland to replenish themselves with food, clothing, and supplies.

September 6. Confederate Generals Lee and Jackson moved into Frederick and Sharpsburg, Maryland. McClellan's Union forces moved northwestward to protect against Confederate attack toward Baltimore and Washington.

September 15. Confederate General Jackson captured Harpers Ferry, taking 12,000 Federal prisoners. McClellan moved westward toward Antietam Creek.

September 16-17. The Battle of Antietam (or Sharpsburg) turned into a Union victory after Lee began to retreat toward Virginia. Frightful losses on both sides.

September 22. Federal troops recaptured Harpers Ferry.

Lincoln made his preliminary announcement for an Emancipation Proclamation. The Union victory at Antietam promised stability and future success for the federal government. By his proclamation, Lincoln set the date of January 1, 1863, as the deadline for all states in rebellion to lay down their arms and return to the Union. If they did not do so, all slaves in such rebellious states would be declared free and the military power of the federal government would be used to provide their freedom.

Late September. Sporadic fighting occurred in Kentucky between forces of Confederate General Bragg and Union Generals Buell and Rosecrans.

September 24. Lincoln temporarily suspended the writ of habeas corpus in federal courts.

September 24-30. General inactivity by McClellan's army which did not pursue Lee retreating into the Shenandoah Valley of Virginia.

October 1-4. Lincoln visited McClellan's army and the battlefield at Antietam. Lincoln set up his "office" next to McClellan's headquarters, conducted his own census of Federal troops (88,095) and concluded that the army wanted to pursue Lee.

October 6. Through General Halleck, Lincoln ordered McClellan to pursue Lee into the Shenandoah Valley. McClellan refused to move.

Late October. Congressional elections showed serious losses for the Republicans. The public was dismayed over federal failure in the Peninsular Campaign and Lincoln's inability to find a winning general.

November 7. Lincoln replaced McClellan with General Ambrose Burnside as commander of the Army of the Potomac. General Lee took up positions behind Fredericksburg, Virginia.

December 1. Lincoln delivered his State of the Union message to the third session of the Thirty-Seventh Congress, stating: "We cannot escape history. We shall nobly save, or meanly lose, the last, best, hope of earth."

December 11. Union forces under General Burnside captured Fredericksburg, Virginia.

December 13. Burnside repeatedly attacked Lee in the Battle of Fredericksburg, suffering staggering losses. Lee held his position. Burnside held Fredericksburg. Federal losses exceeded 12,600. Confederate losses were half as many.

December 15. The Union Army withdrew across the Rappahannock River. The drive toward Richmond had failed.

December 19. A "Cabinet Crisis" developed. Seward and Chase offered to resign in support of Congressional criticism of losses in battle. Lincoln outwitted his critics and brought the government closer together.

Late December. Generals Grant and Sherman in the West continued maneuvers down along the Mississippi River toward Vicksburg.

December 31. Lincoln signed an act of Congress admitting West Virginia into the Union as the 35th State.

1863

January 1. Keeping his promise of 100 days earlier, Lincoln issued the Emancipation Proclamation which freed all slaves in the rebellious areas of the country. He urged black men to abstain from violence and to labor faithfully for wages.

Foreign countries reacted favorably to the Emancipation Proclamation, especially England, France, and Spain.

January 2. The Battle of Murfreesboro, Tennessee, resulted in losses of one-third of all forces on both sides. A succession of other battles in Kentucky and Tennessee seriously drained Confederate manpower and materials.

January 22. The "Burnside Mud March" ended in failure. Winter rains had turned all roads into quagmires in Virginia. Union troops retreated to Fredericksburg.

January 25. Lincoln removed General Burnside from command and placed General Joseph Hooker in command of the Army of the Potomac.

February 25. Lincoln signed Congressional acts to establish a national currency and to establish a National Bank.

March 3. Lincoln approved a draft of manpower for military service.

March. General Hooker prepared to attack Lee in Virginia. General Grant prepared to attack Vicksburg in Mississippi.

April. General Grant's army moved southward bypassing Vicksburg. Admiral Porter's Union Navy sailed down river past Vicksburg.

May 1-4. The Battle of Chancellorsville, Virginia, caused 17,000 casualities to Hooker's Union army, and 12,000 casualities to Lee's Confederate army including the death of General "Stonewall" Jackson. Hooker retreated.

May 4-10. Grant's Union army crosssed the Mississippi River into the state of Mississippi.

May 14. Union forces under Grant captured Jackson, the state capital of Mississippi, and then turned westward toward Vicksburg.

May 18. The siege of Vicksburg began by Grant and Sherman. Confederate General Pemberton became trapped within the city. Also, the Union siege of Port Hudson, Louisiana, began.

June 3. Confederate General Lee began to move his army westward from Fredericksburg, Virginia, preparing to invade the North a second time. Hooker delayed.

June 16. Lee and his forces crossed the Potomac River, northwest of Washington. Hooker was far behind.

June 26. Lee's Confederate army captured Gettysburg, Pennsylvania, and prepared to attack Harrisburg.

June 27. Union General Hooker was replaced by General George Meade with instructions to attack Lee immediately. Lee changed his plans and prepared to meet Meade near Gettysburg.

July 1-3. Furious fighting occurred at the historic Battle of Gettysburg. Union casualties were 23,000 out of 85,000 men. Confederate casualties were 21,000 out of 65,000 troops.

July 4. On this national holiday, July 4, 1863:
First—Lee's Confederate army retreated, badly beaten at the Battle of Gettysburg.
Second—Vicksburg surrendered to General Grant.

July 8. Port Hudson, Louisiana, surrendered to General Banks and his Union forces. The entire Mississippi River was now free.

Mid-July. Lee retreated back into Virginia. Draft riots occurred in New York in protest over excessive casualties in the war. The Copperheads, Democrat peace advocates, grew stronger in the North.

July 26. Confederate Colonel John Morgan and his raiders surrendered in Ohio.

August. The turning point in the war had occurred. The South would grow progressively weaker in manpower, money, and supplies. The North would grow progressively stronger. Minor battles occurred in Virginia, Tennessee, Mississippi, Missouri, and Kansas.

September. Union General Rosecrans and his army moved across northern Alabama toward Chattanooga, Tennessee. Confederate General Bragg retreated to Chickamauga, Georgia.

September 20. Confederate General Bragg won a tactical victory over Union forces at the Battle of Chickamauga.

October. Lincoln placed General Grant in command of the entire Military Division of the Mississippi, including the Departments of the Ohio River, Tennessee River, and Cumberland River. Grant then began preparations for attacks against Chattanooga and Knoxville.

November 19. President Lincoln delivered the immortal Gettysburg Address at the dedication of the famous battlefield.

November 23-25. Union armies attack at Chattanooga.

November 24. The Battle of Lookout Mountain, Tennessee was won by the Union army under General Hooker.

November 25. The Battle of Missionary Ridge was won by Union armies under General Sherman and General Thomas. Confederate General Bragg was thrown into full retreat. Grant then dispatched Sherman's forces to attack General Longstreet at Knoxville, Tennessee.

November 26. The first national Thanksgiving Day was held, as proclaimed by President Lincoln on October 3.

December 6. Arriving to help besieged General Burnside, General Sherman entered Knoxville. Confederate General Longstreet was thrown into full retreat toward eastern Tennessee.

December 8. Addressing Congress, President Lincoln announced his policy of Amnesty and Reconstruction.

Mid-December. Major military campaigning stopped due mainly to severe winter weather.

1864

January. The federal Congress became conscious of the forthcoming national elections. Radical Congressmen demanded punishment of the rebellious Southern states and looked for a presidential candidate who would listen to them. Treasury Secretary Salmon P. Chase became an available candidate with strong Republican support.

February. Lincoln ordered the drafting of 500,000 more Union soldiers. Federal campaigns in Florida and Mississippi gained success. The tactics of Treasury Secretary Chase were exposed by his own supporters and became scandalous.

Early March. Ohio Republicans repudiated the ambitions of Chase and endorsed Lincoln for a second term as president.

March 10. Lincoln appointed General Grant to command all armies of the United States. Grant's success in the Western campaigns overshadowed the criticism of his drinking problem.

Mid-March. In Louisiana, a pro-Union state government took office. In Tennessee, Andrew Johnson became federal military governor.

Late March. General Grant's plans called for General Sherman to march into Georgia to cut off all remaining aid to Virginia, and for himself to lead an assault against Richmond.

March 26. General Grant established his headquarters with General Meade's Army of the Potomac at Culpepper Court House, Virginia.

April. A gigantic buildup of men and war materials occurred for Union and Confederate armies on opposite sides of the Rapidan River in Virginia.

May 5-6. The first two days of the Battle of the Wilderness caused Federal casualties of 18,000 out of 120,000 troops, and Confederate losses of 7,500 out of 60,000. Lee retreated toward Spotsylvania Court House.

May 7. General Sherman with 100,000 Union troops left Tennessee to begin his march on Atlanta, Georgia.

May 8-14. The Battle of Spotsylvania Court House, Virginia, caused 17,500 Union losses out of 110,000 troops. Confederate losses were only half as many but were not replaceable as were Union losses. Lee retreated to Cold Harbor, Virginia, only ten miles from Richmond.

June 1-3. The Battle of Cold Harbor cost about 12,000 Union lives and about 3,000 Confederate lives.

June 8. President Lincoln was nominated for a second term by the National Union Convention at Baltimore, Maryland, supported by most Republicans and some Democrats. Hamlin of Maine was replaced by Andrew Johnson of Tennessee as the nominee for vice-president.

June 15,18. An attack by Federal Union forces on Petersburg, Virginia, failed to capture the city. The siege of Petersburg then began.

June 19. Off the coast of Cherbourg, France, the Union warship *Kearsarge* sank the Confederate warship *Alabama* which had previously sunk or captured sixty-five Union merchant vessels.

June 28. Lincoln signed the congressional act repealing the Fugitive Slave Law.

June 30. Secretary of the Treasury Chase, disappointed over his unsuccessful try for the presidential nomination, opposed administration policies for appointments to various offices. Lincoln accepted his resignation and appointed William P. Fessenden of Maine in his place.

July 4. President Lincoln refused to sign the Wade-Davis Bill which would have enabled Congress to impose conditions and restrictions on the reconstruction of the South.

July 8. The president proclaimed his support for a proposed constitutional amendment abolishing slavery. Also, he refused to set aside the new state governments in Arkansas and Louisiana.

July 9-12. Confederate forces, about 12,000 strong under General Jubal Early, invaded Maryland and the outskirts of Washington, D.C. Federal reinforcements saved the federal Capitol, and General Early retreated into the Shenandoah Valley.

July 17. President Jefferson Davis of the Confederacy appointed General John Hood to replace General Joseph Johnson for the defense of Atlanta, Georgia. With diminishing troops and materials, General Johnson had been able to fight only delaying actions against the advancing Union troops under General Sherman.

July 18. In the face of mounting outrage in the North over severe Federal troop losses in battle, President Lincoln called for 500,000 volunteers to refill army ranks.

July 22. The Battle of Atlanta, Georgia, involved an attack by Confederate forces which lost 10,000 out of 40,000 troops. Federal forces which lost only 4,000, then began a siege of Atlanta.

August 5. The Battle of Mobile Bay, Alabama, was a victory for Admiral Farragut's eighteen Union warships which closed the harbor for any further Confederate use in receiving supplies.

August 6-26. Strategic maneuvering of Federal armies around Petersburg and Richmond, Virginia, included the battles of Weldon Railroad (August 19) and Reams Station (August 25). In Georgia, General Sherman maneuvered west and south of Atlanta cutting off supplies to the city.

August 31. General George B. McClellan was nominated for president by the Democrats meeting in Chicago. George Pendleton of Ohio was nominated for vice-president.

September 1. Confederates evacuated Atlanta, Georgia. The Battle of Jonesborough, Georgia, was a victory for Union forces.

September 19. In the Shenandoah Valley, the Battle of Winchester was a victory for General Sheridan's Union troops.

September 20-29. Minor battles continued around Petersburg and Richmond, Virginia.

October 19. The last major battle in the Shenandoah Valley of Virginia was a vital victory by General Sheridan over Confederate General Early at Cedar Creek.

November 7. The last Confederate congressional session began at Richmond for the Confederate States of America.

November 8. Abraham Lincoln was reelected for a second term. Union victories during August and September (Mobile Bay, Atlanta, Winchester, and Cedar Creek) assured victory for Lincoln.

November 16. General Sherman with 65,000 Union troops left Atlanta to begin his "march to the sea."

November 30. The Battle of Franklin, Tennessee, was a disastrous defeat for Confederate forces that lost over 6,000 men, including six generals, out of 20,000 troops.

December. Winter fighting included steady advance by Sherman's forces across Georgia.

December 5. The thirty-eighth Congress, second

session, of the United States, began with a strong Republican majority in both houses. Radical elements called for revenge against the crumbling Confederacy. Lincoln advocated amnesty.

December 6. President Lincoln delivered his Fourth Annual Message to Congress. He also nominated Salmon P. Chase as chief justice of the U.S. Supreme Court.

December 16. The Battle of Nashville, Tennessee, was a major Union victory of General Thomas over Confederate General Hood. This was the last major battle in the West, as Confederate losses in men and materials could not be replaced.

December 21. Federal troops occupied Savannah, Georgia. On the following day General Sherman sent his famous message to President Lincoln: "I beg to present to you, as a Christmas gift, the City of Savannah."

1865

January 15. Capture of Fort Fisher, North Carolina, by fifty-nine Union naval vessels and 5,000 marines and army troops.

January 19. General Sherman began his march northward into South Carolina.

January 31. The U.S. House of Representatives, by a vote of 119 to 56, passed the Thirteenth Amendment to the Constitution abolishing slavery. It previously had passed the Senate.

General Robert E. Lee was named general-in-chief of all Confederate armies.

February 1. Illinois became the first state to ratify the thirteenth amendment. By December 18, 1865, the necessary two-thirds of the states had ratified the amendment and it became law.

February 3. At Hampton Roads, Virginia, aboard the River Queen, a conference was held regarding a negotiated peace. President Lincoln and Secretary of State Seward represented the Union; Vice-President Alexander Stephens and John Hunter represented the Confederacy. Terms could not be agreed upon for an armistice.

February 17. Federal forces under General Sherman captured Columbia, the capital of South Carolina. Also, Charleston, where the war began at Fort Sumter, was evacuated by the Confederates.

February 22. Federal troops captured Wilmington, North Carolina, the last major port in the South.

March 4. Abraham Lincoln was inaugurated into his second term as president. At the ceremony in Washington, D.C., Lincoln's famous Second Inaugural Address included the words, "With malice toward none; with Charity for all;"

March 18. The Confederate Congress adjourned, never to meet again.

March 21. The Battle of Bentonville, North Carolina, was the last serious effort by the Confederates to stop the advance of General Sherman who now had over 100,000 troops. Confederate General Johnson, who had replaced General Hood, retreated northward toward Virginia to try to join up with General Lee.

March 24. President Lincoln arrived at City Point,

Virginia, on the James River, Headquarters of General Grant.

March 27-28. Meetings were held by President Lincoln with General Grant, General Sherman, and Admiral Porter on the Admiral's flagship to discuss: 1. Surrender terms for the Confederate armies; 2. Lincoln's Executive Plan of Reconstruction with Amnesty for the South.

March 29-31. Skirmishes against Petersburg and Richmond foretold a major federal offensive.

April 1. The final attack by General Lee against Union forces at Five Forks was a severe defeat for the Confederacy.

President Lincoln remained at City Point. By this date, all Union armies together included over 1,000,000 troops. All Confederate armies together had shrunk to fewer than 100,000 troops.

April 2. The Confederate government evacuated Richmond. The burning of Richmond was begun by retreating Confederate forces.

April 3 (Monday). Federal troops under General Weitzel occupied Richmond, former capital of the Confederacy.

Federal troops also captured Petersburg where major destruction was averted. Here, President Lincoln visited General Grant and reviewed federal troops in the afternoon.

General Lee retreated toward Appomattox. Confederate President Davis set up his office at Danville.

April 4 (Tuesday). President Lincoln visited the burning city of Richmond to begin implementing his policy of Reconstruction with Amnesty. To General Weitzel he suggested: "If I were in your place, General, I'd let 'em up easy; let 'em up easy."

April 5 (Wednesday). For a second day, Lincoln came ashore from the U.S.S. *Malvern* to Richmond. He conferred with Judge John A. Campbell regarding a possible meeting of the Virginia state legislature to recall its state militia from the war and to restore national authority. Then he returned to City Point.

April 6 (Thursday). The last major engagement in· Virginia between Confederate and Union Troops occurred at Saylors Creek where 8,000 Confederates surrendered.

At City Point, President Lincoln wrote letters further stating procedures for defeated states rejoining the Union.

April 7 (Friday). General Grant began correspondence with General Lee suggesting surrender of Confederate forces because of "the hopelessness of further resistance" and in order to prevent "any further effusion of blood."

At City Point, President Lincoln sent numerous letters and telegrams, including instructions for the plans for raising the Union Flag over Fort Sumter in Charleston Harbor, South Carolina, the date to be April 14, 1865.

April 8 (Saturday). Lincoln departed from City Point aboard the River Queen to return to Washington, D.C. where Secretary of State Seward had been injured seriously in a carriage accident.

Generals Grant and Lee exchanged communications.

April 9 (Palm Sunday before Easter). At dawn near Appomattox Station, Virginia, Confederate forces made a faint attempt to break out of their growing encirclement, and quickly realized the futility of their attack.

In the early afternoon, at the home of Wilmer McLean at Appomattox Court House, Virginia, General Lee accepted General Grant's lenient terms for the surrender of the Confederate Army of Northern Virginia.

In the early evening, President Lincoln arrived back in Washington, D.C. News of Lee's surrender spread quickly throughout the Northern states.

April 10 (Monday). Victory celebrations began in all Northern cities and towns. Swamped with serenaders, President Lincoln promised to speak on the evening of the following day.

Confederate President Jefferson Davis and his cabinet departed by train from Danville to go to Greensborough, North Carolina.

April 11 (Tuesday). Victory celebrations intensified in the North. General Sherman fought several small battles in advancing toward Goldsborough, North Carolina.

In the evening, from a window of the White House, President Lincoln delivered his last public address, a so-called Victory Speech which stressed bringing the Southern states back into the Union under a policy of reconstruction with amnesty.

April 12 (Wednesday). General Sherman advanced toward Raleigh, North Carolina, where Confederate General Johnson's Army was mainly intact. At Greensborough, North Carolina, Jefferson Davis argued with his cabinet whether or not his remaining Confederate armies should surrender or try for a negotiated peace.

In Washington, President Lincoln wrote to General Weitzel not to allow the Virginia Legislature to meet since Lee had already surrendered. Radical members of Congress protested to Lincoln against his policy of amnesty.

April 13 (Thursday). General Sherman's Union Army entered Raleigh, North Carolina.

Public rejoicing in the Northern states increased, with normal business almost coming to a standstill.

In addition to his heavy schedule of meetings, President Lincoln wrote six messages including a Memorandum Respecting Reduction of the Regular Army which he gave to Stanton. On the basis of this memorandum, Stanton as secretary of war, issued an order to stop the drafting of citizens for service in the armed forces.

April 14 (Good Friday before Easter). This day will remain historic as long as the history of mankind remains. In Washington, D.C., the day began with beautiful spring sunshine. Dogwood trees and lilacs were in blossom. People were happy. The great American Civil War was over!

In the morning, Lincoln's son, Lieutenant

Robert Todd Lincoln, returned to the White House from Appomattox. Before noon General Grant attended the President's cabinet meeting. Secretary of the Navy Welles wrote in his diary that the president was adamant about reconstruction with amnesty. Welles quoted Lincoln as saying; "We must extinguish our resentment if we expect harmony and union."

The day was an unofficial day of national celebration. In an impressive ceremony, the Union Flag was raised over Fort Sumter in Charleston Harbor, South Carolina.

Afternoon office work was interrupted long enough for the president to take Mrs. Lincoln for a carriage ride. Evening dinner was delayed by additional meetings and messages.

At 8:30 p.m. the president and his wife Mary departed from the White House to attend Laura Keen's stage play *Our American Cousin* at Ford's Theater.

At 10:30 p.m. President Lincoln was shot in the back of the head by John Wilkes Booth. Mortally wounded, the president was carried across the street from the theater to the home of William Peterson where an all-night vigil was held by cabinet members, Congressmen, family, and friends.

April 15 (Saturday). At 7:22 a.m. President Abraham Lincoln died. To those who were gathered around the bed, Secretary of War Stanton was heard to say: "Now he belongs to the ages."

April 21-May 3. Lincoln's funeral train traveled from Washington, D.C. to Springfield, Illinois.

May 4. Abraham Lincoln was buried in Oak Ridge Cemetery, Springfield, Illinois.

Selected References

More than 5,000 books and pamphlets have been written about Abraham Lincoln. To list only a few recommended books for admirers of Lincoln would be to omit many books that ought to be included. The following, then, represents only the arbitrary preferences of this author, and in no way denies the importance of the books not listed.

For a single volume, factually accurate and clearly written, special notice must be given to:

Thomas, Benjamin P. *Abraham Lincoln: A Biography*. New York: Alfred A. Knopf, 1952.

For the student who wishes to analyze the complete public addresses, informal speeches, letters, telegrams, proclamations, and other writings and messages of Lincoln, the most authentic source is:

Basler, Roy P., ed. *The Collected Works of Abraham Lincoln*, 9 volumes. New Brunswick, New Jersey: Rutgers University Press, 1953.

Other references recommended for general reading on Abraham Lincoln include:

Angle, Paul M. *A Shelf of Lincoln Books: A Critical Selective Bibliography*. New Brunswick, New Jersey: Rutgers University Press, 1946.

Basler, Roy P., ed. *The Collected Works of Abraham Lincoln: Supplement, 1832-1865*. Westport, Conn.: Greenwood Press, 1974.

Beveridge, Albert J. *Abraham Lincoln, 1809-1858*. 2 volumes, Boston and New York: Houghton Mifflin Company, 1928. Library edition, Boston and New York: Houghton Mifflin Company, 1928. 4 volumes.

Charnwood, Godfrey Rathbone Benson, Lord. *Abraham Lincoln*. London: Constable & Company, Ltd., 1916. New Edition, New York: Pocket Boods, Inc. 1951.

Herndon, William H., and Weik, Jesse William. *Herndon's Lincoln: The True Story of a great Life* 3 volumes. Chicago: Belford, Clark & Company, 1889, New Edition, with an introduction and notes by Paul M. Angle; Illustrated with photographs from the Meserve Collection, Cleveland and New York: The World Publishing Company, 1949.

Long, E.B. *The Civil War Day by Day: An Almanac, 1861-1865*. Garden City, New York: Double Day & Company, Inc. 1971.

Lorant, Stephan. *Lincoln: His Life in Photographs*. New York: Duell, Sloan and Pearce, 1941. Revised and enlarged edition, *Lincoln, A Picture Story of His Life*. New York: Harper & Brothers, 1957.

Monaghan, Jay. *Lincoln Bibliography, 1830-1939*. 2 volumes. Springfield, Illinois: Illinois State Historical Library, 1943.

Diplomat in Carpet Slippers: Abraham Lincoln Deals with Foreign Affairs. Indianapolis and New York: the Bobbs-Merrill Company, 1945.

Nicolay, John George, and John Hay. *Abraham Lincoln: A History*. 10 volumes. New York: The Century Company, 1890, 1914.

Tarbell, Ida Minerva. *The Life of Abraham Lincoln*. 2 volumes. New York: The Doubleday and McClure Company, 1900. Revised edition, New York: The Macmillian Company, 1928, 2 volumes.

Welles, Gideon, *Diary of Gideon-Welles: Secretary of the Navy Under Lincoln and Johnson*. 3 volumes. Boston and New York: Houghton Mifflin Company, 1911. New Edition, 3 volumes, New York: W.W. Norton & Co. 1960.

Index

Dresser, Charles, 52, 96, 103

Early, Jubal, 120, 121
Edwards, Mrs. Ninian, 102
Edwardsville, Illinois, 32
Eighth Judicial Circuit, Illinois 52, 102
Electoral College, 110
Elizabeth City County, Virginia, 87
Elizabethtown, Kentucky, 52, 97, 98
Elwood, Kansas, 109
Emancipation Memorial, 33
Emancipation of slaves, 8, 33, 34, 48, 54, 61, 69, 86, 87, 92, 115, 116, 117
Episcopal Church, Springfield, Illinois, 52, 103
Everett, Edward, 110
Exeter, New Hampshire, 109

Fair Oaks, Battle of, 115
Farewell Address, 18, 29, 53, 69, 85, 111
Farmington, Kentucky, 102
Farragut, David, 114, 121
Federal Government of the United States, 80, 81, 82, 83, 84
Federal Income Tax Law, 115
Federal territories, 24, 26, 80, 81, 82, 83
Fell, Jesse, 109
Fessenden, William P., 120
Few, William, 81, 82
Fillmore, Millard, 107

First Inaugural Address, 33, 53, 61, 90, 111
Fitzsimmons, Thomas, 81
Five Forks, Battle of, 64, 122
Florida (Confederate battleship), 64
Florida, State of, 87, 89, 110, 111
Ford's Theater, Washington, D.C., 67, 125
Fort Donelson, Tennessee, 113
Fort Fisher, North Carolina, 122
Fort Henry, Tennessee, 113
Fort Pilaski, Georgia, 114
Fortress Monroe, Virginia, 114, 115
Fort Sumter, South Carolina, 64, 66, 111, 112, 122, 123, 124
Fourth Annual Message to Congress, 121
France, 117
Franklin, Tennessee (Battle of), 121
Frayser's Farm, Virginia (Battle of), 115
Frederick, Maryland, 116
Fredericksburg, Virginia, 27, 117, 118
Freeport, Illinois, 4, 24, 47, 108
Free-soilers, 106
Free-State Constitutions, 85
Fremont, John C., 36, 106, 107, 112, 113
French, Daniel C., 58
Fugitive Slave Law, 4, 33, 46, 111, 120

Gaine's Mill, Virginia (Battle of), 115
Galesburg Debate, 24, 25, 47, 108
Gardner, Alexander, 50
Garrison, William Lloyd, 66
General Land Office, 105
General War Order Number One, 113
Gentry, Allen, 99
Gentryville, Indiana, 52, 98, 99
Georgia, State of, 64, 81, 87, 89, 110, 111, 114, 120, 122
Gettysburg Address, 19, 21, 29, 48, 69, 87, 88, 119
Gettysburg, Pennsylvania (Battle of), 35, 36, 59, 87, 118
Gilman, Nicholas, 81
Globe Tavern, 103
God, 19, 34, 36, 45, 48, 51, 52, 53, 54, 55, 56, 65, 86, 87, 88, 89, 91, 92
Goldsborough, North Carolina, 124
Golden Rule, 54, 62
Good Friday, April 14, 1865, 66, 67, 124
Grant, Ulysses S., 18, 19, 50, 59, 64, 65, 66, 92, 113, 114, 115, 117, 118, 119, 120, 122, 123, 124
Great Britain, 113
Great Debates, 46, 117
Greely, Horace, 8, 21, 34, 104, 116
Greensborough, North Carolina, 124

Greenwood Press, 126
Grigsby, Aaron, 99
Grigsby, Charles, 99
Grimshaw's *History of the United States*, 99
Gurley, Phineas D., 54

Habeas Corpus, Writ of, 34, 35, 36
Half-face camp, 98
Halleck, Henry W., 5, 115, 116, 117
Hamilton, Charles, 127
Hamilton, Ohio, 109
Hamlin, Hannibal, 104, 110, 120
Hampton Roads, Virginia, 122
Hanks, Dennis, 98
Hanks, John, 99
Hanks, Nancy, 97
Hardin County, Kentucky, 97
Hardin, John J., 103
Harper's Ferry, West Virginia, 84, 109, 116
Harris, Ira, 65
Harrisburg, Pennsylvania, 118
Harrison, William Henry, 102
Harrison's Landing, Virginia, 115
Hartford, Connecticut, 109
Hay, John, 28, 91, 127
Hazel, Caleb, 98
Henry, James M., 80
Herndon, William H., 4, 22, 103, 126
Hesler, Alexander, 20
Hodges, Albert G., 35, 36
Hodgensville, Kentucky, 97